MW00979155

Canada's Technology Triangle

An Economic Celebration

Produced in cooperation with the Economic Development
In Canada's Technology Triangle Inc.

CANADA'S TECHNOLOGY TRIANGLE

An Economic Celebration

By JERRY AMERNIC
CORPORATE PROFILES BY GARY NYP
FEATURING THE PHOTOGRAPHY OF MIKE GRANDMAISON

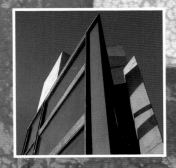

Canada's Technology Triangle:
An Economic Celebration

by Jerry Amernic
Corporate Profiles by Gary Nyp
Featuring the photography of Mike Grandmaison

Community Communications, Inc.
Publishers: Ronald P. Beers and James E. Turner

Staff for *Canada's Technology Triangle:*
An Economic Celebration

Publisher's Sales Associates:	BRIAN RHODES
	DAVID McKINNEY
Executive Editor:	JAMES E. TURNER
Senior Editor:	MARY SHAW HUGHES
Managing Editor:	KURT R. NILAND
Profile Editors:	KARI COLLIN JARNOT AND
	MARY CATHERINE RICHARDSON
Editorial Assistants:	ANNE SHINN AND
	MANDY LUNSFORD
Design Director:	SCOTT PHILLIPS
Designer:	EDDIE LAVOIE
Photo Editors:	KURT R. NILAND
	AND EDDIE LAVOIE
Production Manager:	JARROD STIFF
Contract Managers:	KATRINA WILLIAMS
	AND CHRISTI STEVENS
National Sales Manager:	JOHN HECKER
Sales Assistant:	ANNETTE R. LOZIER
Proofreader:	WYNONA B. HALL,
	KARI COLLIN JARNOT
Accounting Services:	SARA ANN TURNER

CCI

Community Communications, Inc.
Montgomery, Alabama

James E. Turner, Chairman of the Board
Ronald P. Beers, President
Daniel S. Chambliss, Vice President

© 1999 Community Communications
All Rights Reserved
Published 1999
Printed in USA
First Edition
Library of Congress Catalog Number: 99-31722
ISBN: 1-885352-91-3

Every effort has been made to ensure the accuracy of the information herein. However,
the authors and Community Communications are not responsible for any errors or
omissions which might have occurred.

CONTENTS

Foreword, 9

Preface 11

Part One, 12

Photos on pages 2, 4, 6, 8, 10, 12, 14, 77, 98 by Mike Grandmaison

CONTENTS

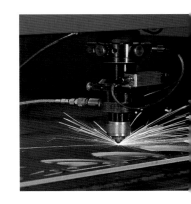

FOREWORD

Economic Development in Canada's Technology Triangle Inc. is committed to fostering vibrant and sustainable economic development for its citizens. The term "Canada's Technology Triangle" is also used to identify a physical location that is the gateway to the industrial heartland of Southern Ontario. What brings everyone together and allows everything to work in concert is that Canada's Technology Triangle is an attitude as much as it is a place. The view that is unquestionably shared by its residents is that we live and work in a great place. Both families and businesses have established themselves in an environment of economic diversity and corporate excellence.

Canada's Technology Triangle has grown over time on a foundation of tradition, culture and entrepreneurship that has transcended all challenges and changes. From traditional farmer's markets to leading-edge technologies, we are proud of our successes and eagerly look forward to the future and continued prosperity. In fact, we invite you to join us as we continue on a journey that has been both exciting and rewarding.

Over the years, our accomplishments have been many and we appreciate that a great deal of our development can be attributed to the many partnerships within the private and public sectors. We value, and so will create and nurture, strong mutually supportive relationships with our stakeholders. We cherish entrepreneurial people, enterprise, investment and innovation. We value all human ability.

As an economic development organization, we hope that this publication will provide you with a sense of our community and what we are fortunate to enjoy and share. We are proud to introduce you to Canada's Technology Triangle.

Rick Thompson
Executive Director
Economic Development In Canada's Technology Triangle Inc.

PREFACE

It really is the best of both worlds and that, not surprisingly, was one of the prime reasons behind the formation of Canada's Technology Triangle (CTT) in the first place. CTT is two things: a region and an actual organization. CTT is a unique geographical area at the centre of Canada's business and industrial heartland, encompassing the urban communities of Cambridge, Guelph, Kitchener, Waterloo, and the Regional Municipality of Waterloo. This area is home to some 500,000 people and a workforce of about 260,000 people. But it isn't just any workforce.

Indeed, within CTT are three world-class universities and a community college. Add in a healthy, diversified economy boasting an international reputation in such areas as technology and agri-business, not to mention extensive research and development facilities and a strong service sector, and you have a combination that's hard to beat. When it comes to location, education and technology, this area just may be without peer. Consider this: the province of Ontario is the economic engine that drives the Canadian economy, but since 1984, CTT has grown nearly twice as quickly as the province itself!

CTT, the organization, was formed through an innovative idea involving the Economic Development Departments of the area's four cities. Back in 1987 the respective Economic Development Officers decided to pool their attributes and share services. A steering committee was formed and 10 years later CTT—an independent organization—was born.

The partners of CTT are the Cities of Cambridge, Guelph, Kitchener, Waterloo and the Regional Municipality of Waterloo.

Each member brings its own individual attributes to the mix. The metropolitan areas of Kitchener and Waterloo, has 10,000 businesses, is one of the fastest-growing urban centres in Canada.

Guelph and Cambridge are cities of roughly 100,000 people each. Some of the world's leading and award-winning manufacturing, industrial and high-technology companies have selected Cambridge as their headquarters while Guelph provides a highly desirable investment and business opportunity for new companies.

The Regional Municipality of Waterloo which incorporated in 1973 to replace the County of Waterloo, features a unique mix of rural, suburban and urban communities which together offer one of the highest standards of living in Canada, if not the world. The regional government allows for efficiencies in providing community-wide services across various area municipal boundaries.

The respective Chambers of Commerce are devoted to creating jobs and contributing to what is already widely regarded as a fine quality of life. Their combined 3,000 members, who reflect CTT's widely diversified economic base, are served by hundreds of volunteers and staff addressing business needs, interests, issues and concerns.

Taken as one, they represent CTT. Canada's Technology Triangle. An entity that truly is one of the most prosperous and blessed anywhere.

— Jerry Amernic

PART ONE

*An Economic
Celebration*

CHAPTER ONE

Echoes of the Past 1

Doon Heritage Crossroads is really a photograph. Depicting a rural Waterloo County community from the year 1914, it offers a snapshot of life from back then—and it was an exciting time, to be sure. A revolutionary invention, the automobile, was beginning to replace the horse and buggy. Electricity was lighting up homes and factories. George V was King, and Canada, with the advent of the Great War, was about to embark on a new coming of age as a nation. The farms, homes and businesses of that remarkable age all come alive at Doon Heritage on Homer Watson Boulevard in Kitchener.

Doon Heritage Crossroads presents a snapshot of life as it was in early twentieth-century Waterloo County. *Photo by Mike Grandmaison*

Wagons, tools and utensils, furniture and other antiquities left behind by the pioneers form the remarkable collection at Doon Heritage. *Photo by Mike Grandmaison*

The popular attraction is considered something of a domain of riches and artifacts that could easily fill a museum; but there is no such facility here. Over the years, many families from the area have made contributions, and everything is being stored for the day when a museum can be opened and all of this can be displayed.

The vivid recreation of life from 1914 aside, Doon Heritage is a large holding site. There are four storage vaults with bibles and religious texts, some dating back to the late 1600s. There are conservation laboratories for historic objects made of wood, metal, paper and textiles. But the most remarkable section of all is a huge room—it's more like a warehouse—where pioneer utensils and furniture sit quietly. A wagon that could have belonged to the first Mennonite family who made the long trek from Pennsylvania Dutch country sleeps listlessly as do the countless reminders of everyday life from the first pioneers.

The items in this remarkable collection come from all over the former Waterloo County. In 1853 the county officially came into being as a political entity, bringing together five townships and two villages. On January 1, 1973, it was no more, disappearing into the newly created Regional Municipality of Waterloo. And while the communities that comprise the region all hail from the same historic womb, the story behind each one of them is just a little bit different.

Mennonite vendors in today's CTT live and work much like the area's early settlers. *Photo by Mike Grandmaison*

The city of Cambridge was created in 1973 when three municipalities—Preston, Galt and Hespeler—merged as a means of overcoming some common problems. This was not an easy thing to do as each was a distinct and independent entity that had developed over a period of almost 200 years. However, one larger city obviously would have that much greater critical mass.

In its early days, Galt (named in honour of John Galt, the Scottish novelist and Commissioner of the Canada Company), was almost exclusively an agrarian community serving the needs of farmers in the surrounding countryside. By the late 1830s an industrial base emerged, and the city began to develop an industrial base. Galt's reputation for quality manufacturing eventually earned it the nickname "The Manchester of Canada," and it remained one of the largest and most important towns in the area for several decades.

Jacob Hespeler, for whom the town of Hespeler was eventually named, purchased 145 acres along the Speed River and built an industrial complex there that provided the foundation for the settlement's later industrial strength. Despite its small size, Hespeler contained one of the largest textile manufacturers in all of Canada. After World War II, however, the Canadian textile industry fell into a steady decline and Hespeler could no longer compete in the world market. Although the town was successful in attracting some new businesses, it remained in the shadow of the larger neighbouring town and cities.

John Erb was among the first settlers who arrived in what was later to become the town of Preston. Having acquired 7,500 acres of land where the Grand and Speed Rivers meet, Erb and his wife built a sawmill and grist mill on the banks of the Speed River. The grist mill has milled flour continuously since its construction in 1807 to the present day, and it is recognized as one of the oldest continuously operating industrial sites in Canada. After Erb's death in 1832 the lands to the south of the Speed River were sold to commercial interests, immediately attracting a

Downtown Cambridge straddles the Grand River in the Old Galt section of town. *Photo by Mike Grandmaison*

number of tradesmen, artisans and craftsmen, most of them from Germany. Preston, in fact, attracted more Europeans than any other village in the area, but it wasn't until 1900 that the population broke the 2,000 barrier with the installation of the railway.

As with other jurisdictions in the area, like Kitchener and Waterloo, Cambridge made sure to hang onto its past. A key plank in the new, larger community was the contin-

ued presence of the three former downtown cores of the three founding municipalities.

Today, downtown Cambridge straddles the Grand River in the Old Galt section and has grown to become a centre for commerce and retail. Also, there is a specially designated district for factory outlets. Hespeler Village, meanwhile, is a core of service, commerce and retail businesses beside the historic Speed River. Finally, the Preston Town

The city of Cambridge formed with the mering of three municipalities, Preston, Galt and Hespeler. The city's 200-year old charm is still evident with its historical homes and churches.
Photo by Mike Grandmaison

Centre is distinguished by the wide boulevard of King Street and is an active centre of shopping and commerce. Hespeler Road also continued to develop as a busy hub with a wide variety of retail and service businesses anchored by the Cambridge Centre, which is a modern regional mall.

Cambridge today is a city of 100,000 people that enjoys a healthy and diversified economic base. The range of businesses include automotive, traditional and advanced manufacturing, agriculture, financial services, insurance, science and technology. The world-class corporations who have set up shop here include the likes of Toyota, Rockwell, Babcock & Wilcox, Hostess, Frito-Lay and Penmans. The workforce is 50,000 strong and a full third of them are engaged in manufacturing.

GUELPH

After the American Revolutionary War of 1776-1783, British Loyalists and their Indian allies, the Iroquois, were driven north into Canada. The British not only granted the Iroquois a strip of land on both sides of the Grand River, but agreed to give the Mississauga Indians a large tract of land that included what is now Guelph.

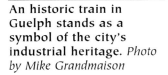

An historic train in Guelph stands as a symbol of the city's industrial heritage. *Photo by Mike Grandmaison*

Guelph Township was acquired by the government as early as 1792, but it wouldn't be settled by the white man for another 35 years. It was founded in 1827 by John Galt, a Scottish writer and businessman who four years earlier had organized the Canada Company. This organization had incredible powers; it could purchase, hold, improve, settle and dispose of waste or other lands, make advances of capital to settlers and make improvements to roads.

From those beginnings emerged a village. In 1840 Wellington District was created and with it Guelph became the District Town. Throughout the balance of the 19th century, Guelph expanded into a successful community in its own right. The local economy was one of farmers, merchants, millers, manufacturers and assorted busi-

Guelph today is an attractive community that is well known for its rich architectural heritage, vibrant cultural life and picturesque natural setting. *Photo by Mike Grandmaison*

nessmen. Industrialization and the coming of the railway further contributed to Guelph's growth. In 1879 the town became a city and separated from the County of Wellington. The first high school was built in 1887, but it was the School of Agriculture and the Experimental Farm, dedicated to improving agricultural production, that would eventually achieve renown far and wide. By the turn of the century, the Agricultural School had forged an impressive reputation and eventually expanded its course of study to the college level. On July 6, 1864, Guelph even achieved national attention with the running of the

(above) The city of Guelph, seen here from the Cutten Club Golf Course, is admired for its beautiful parks and trails, rivers and rolling hills. *Photo by Mike Grandmaison*

(left) Guelph City Hall. *Photo by Mike Grandmaison*

Queen's Plate horse race at the mile track of Gray's Inn on Eramosa Road. The Queen's Plate isn't merely the foremost horse race in Canada, it is North America's oldest annually held sporting event.

Photo by Mike Grandmaison

The 330-hectare University of Guelph, named as one of Ontario's "elite six" by the *Toronto Sun*, has been internationally recognized for its general academic excellence and for its leadership in the field of agricultural economics and business. The university also takes pride in its dynamic balance of student-centred environment, extensive research and community outreach. Like the other universities in CTT, the University of Guelph remains intrinsically tied to the surrounding community.

Today, modern Guelph is an attractive community that is well known for its rich architectural heritage, vibrant cultural life and picturesque natural setting at the junction of the Speed and Eramosa Rivers. Its century-old limestone buildings and downtown avenues are set in natural surroundings of beautiful parks and trails, rivers and rolling hills, all of it a splendid mix of the old and the new.

One of the most remarkable sides of Guelph is its extensive park system and outdoor recreation facilities. According to the city, it provides and maintains over 100 parks throughout the city, and maintains more than 528 hectares (1300 acres) of open space.

But its abundance of parks and trees isn't the only reason the city has no trouble seeing green. Guelph also has become something of an international star in the world of agri-business, much the same way Waterloo has established a reputation as a leader in the field of computer technology. Considering its rich agrarian heritage and its access to high technology, it is not surprising that most of Ontario's multi-billion-dollar food business sector is located in and around Guelph.

KITCHENER

It was known far and wide as "Canada's German capital" until such a designation was deemed no longer appropriate. Kitchener, originally known as Berlin, would eventually grow into the industrial heart of Canada's Technology Triangle. Along with Waterloo, it was rooted in a simple time by a unique and most unpretentious people: the Mennonites. It was late in the 18th century when control of the region that would become Waterloo County started to pass from the hands of the natives who had been there for centuries, to the white man. These were Six

Mild mid-summer afternoons and evenings allow Guelph residents and visitors a chance to dine outdoors. *Photo by Mike Grandmaison*

Nations Indian lands, 12 miles wide along the length of the Grand River. The Mennonites were a people who didn't embrace the new industrial values of British North America, preferring to hang onto the vestiges of a traditional lifestyle.

They started coming from Pennsylvania at the turn of the century. Ezra Erb, Waterloo Township's first historian, described the experience of seven families who came from Montgomery County in 1802:

"The most extraordinary difficulties beset them while crossing the Alleghany Mountains with their heavily laden teams. They found it necessary to unload a considerable portion of their baggage and goods, and pay for their conveyance, their own teams being utterly unable to bring all across. They crossed the Niagara River on what was then called 'flats.' There was no accident nor sickness on this trip. The time required in coming from Montgomery County to Waterloo County was 10 weeks, including the two weeks which they laid over at Horning's on the mountain while the men in the company worked on the road through the Beverly Swamp, making it so that horseteams in some way could be taken over it."

In 1805 the German Company of Lancaster County purchased two-thirds of the then fledgling township, and the lands were eventually cleared into 200-acre farms. The original settlers were soon joined by Roman Catholics and Lutherans who hailed from German communities of Europe. Pioneers from the British Isles came as well. These people were an organized lot who respected the principles of democracy. The first council of the new County of Waterloo met at the courthouse in Berlin on January 24, 1853, but the town didn't achieve this status without a fight from the larger village of Galt. Council meetings were often lively, raucous affairs with debates not only between villages, but between the farmers and manufacturers too.

Kitchener was settled by more and more German immigrants who brought with them their traditional skills—leatherwork, brewing and furniture-making. They prospered and by the middle of the 19th century a solid network of roads was established. Then, in the 1850s, the railways arrived. The railways were a major catalyst to economic progress in the entire region. Indeed, this was a booming industrial age, with the township's rural population peaking in 1861. Ten years later, in 1871, Berlin achieved the political status of a town and manufacturing interests took off; the census of Waterloo County that year showed that most business enterprises were small craftshops: blacksmiths, tinsmiths, bakers, saddlers, shoemakers, tailors, carpenters and carriage and wagon makers.

Originally called "Berlin," the thriving city of Kitchener is known as Canada's "German Capital." *Photo by Mike Grandmaison*

The pulse of downtown Kitchener can be measured by its exciting cityscape and cultural events. *Photo by Mike Grandmaison*

Victoria Park in Kitchener is one of the many parks.
Photo by Mike Grandmaison

One of the legends of the time was Jacob D. Shoemaker. He was born in 1799 in Montgomery County, and managed three farms in the new American republic before migrating to Waterloo Township, along with his extended family, in 1829. Eventually, he bought 224 acres of land in the southwest part of the township and lived there until his death in 1902—at the ripe old age of 103. At the centennial family reunions organized by Mennonite founding families, there was always much talk about Shoemaker and his many offspring.

In the late 1800s Berlin's population grew by 170 percent and by 1891 was even with its rival, Galt. Berlin wore its German heritage with pride, which made it markedly different from such towns as Guelph, Brantford and London, all of them staunchly British. But the First World War wrought changes and the people of Berlin were forced to take a long look at just who they were.

By 1912 Berlin had further solidified an identity and its name when it became a city, prompting its withdrawal from the county system. But four years later the decision was made to change the name to Kitchener, after a famous British warrior, and this effectively divided the community. In fact, those years immediately following the war were difficult and introspective ones for its citizens. However, the 1920s were a time of new communications and education as the traditional differences amongst the peoples in the region started to disappear. It was then that Kitchener became more like the rest of Ontario.

There was no mistaking allegiances in World War II as Kitchener rallied to the Canadian and Allied cause. During the war, 131 women from Kitchener joined the Armed Forces. It was a time when women were demonstrating their significant contribution to not only defence, but business as well; more than 2,500 women from Kitchener and Waterloo entered the workforce in the war years.

According to its mission statement, "Kitchener is a City that builds upon its proud traditions and progressive community leadership to remain one of the most vibrant, prosperous and livable communities in Canada." Pictured here is City Hall.
Photo by Mike Grandmaison

After the war, Kitchener joined in the great economic boom that engulfed central Ontario and the rest of the country; But still, acceptance of the area's historical heritage remained. In

1946 the Canadian Society for German Relief was formed to help the often difficult transition of ethnic Germans from war-torn Europe to the local area. Five years later another organization, the Trans-Canada Alliance of German Canadians, was formed and there was an immediate reawakening in German pride. This was much in evidence in the 1960s when "multiculturalism" became an official policy of Canada; Kitchener quickly got on the ethnic bandwagon by establishing the annual Oktoberfest, a celebration that grew into a major tourist attraction.

WATERLOO

Waterloo, though growing alongside Kitchener, did not face the same hardships of identity and the somewhat uninhibited immersion into mainstream Canadian life that was experienced by Kitchener. Prominent Waterloo politicians of the mid-19th century were Daniel Snyder, Moses Springer and John Hoffman. In fact, it was Hoffman's survey of the 1850s that effectively laid out the city. Surprisingly, the physical size of Waterloo hasn't changed much since that time.

Waterloo did grow, however, from incorporation as a village in 1857 to a town in 1876, and finally to a full-fledged city in 1948. Companies like Seagrams, Mutual Life and Dominion Life grew and prospered as Waterloo became a centre for the insurance industry. Waterloo's first subdivision came to fruition in the late 1950s, but the move into this new age of development didn't occur without strong links to the city's past. When the former 100-acre Seagram Stables were being developed into the city's first shopping plaza, one stable remained so as not to destroy a piece of history. Indeed, even in 1960, a time when progress and development were the order of the day, Waterloo boasted more horse-drawn traffic than any other city in Ontario.

This was the year that construction began on Waterloo Square, which was the catalyst for Waterloo's multimillion-dollar downtown shopping development on King Street. The prediction was made that the heart of the city would beat with renewed vigour, and it did. The city had been in a depression. A 1960 market survey showed that Waterloo residents conducted only 25 per cent of their shopping in the city while 50 per cent was done in Kitchener. The new development, of course, changed all that.

Kitchener's quaint neighborhoods exhibit a wonderful blend of old- and new-world styles.
Photo by Mike Grandmaison

(above) As dusk fades to twilight, Waterloo's skyline sparkles. *Photo by Mike Grandmaison*

(left) Sunrise casts an awakening glow on the streets of downtown Waterloo. *Photo by Mike Grandmaison*

(opposite page) Abraham Erb's Grist Mill in Waterloo stands as a reminder of the region's early days. *Photo by Mike Grandmaison*

Waterloo has since carved for itself a worldwide reputation as a centre of education and technology with two leading universities inside its boundaries—the University of Waterloo and Wilfrid Laurier University. In terms of business and industry, Waterloo is a blend of the old and the new as many of the family enterprises that began in the early 1800s continue to thrive alongside the new, high-technology ventures that began to flourish in the 1980s.

The key to Waterloo's enduring success has been its diversified economy. The central business section, known to locals as Uptown Waterloo, provides the best of both city and country life in a way that most communities can only dream about. The small-city shopping mall is surrounded by specialty shops, restaurants, hotels and heritage attractions that go back to the original Mennonite settlers. The industrial parks in the north end of the city have become an internationally recognized centre for high-technology pursuits, many of them connected to the University of Waterloo. This new sector has mixed well with the more traditional manufacturing and service elements of the economy.

WATERLOO REGION

The Regional Municipality of Waterloo was formed in 1973 as a partnership between seven area cities and townships: the cities of Cambridge, Kichener, and Waterloo, and the townships of North Dumfries, Wellesley, Wilmot, and Woolwich. This structure of government allows for a more efficient and co-operative dispensation of services across municipal boundaries. Such community-wide services include a common water supply and wastewater treatment, waste management (landfill sites, recycling, and garbage collection), community health, social services (welfare assistance, child care, employment programs), regional planning, social housing, regional roads, traffic signals and transit, township libraries, two museums, a Regional airport, ambulance services and emergency planning.

(above) Started in 1844 by David Kuntz, Kuntz Brewery was one likely result of German immigration to the Waterloo area. Visitors can enjoy the gardens maintained by the famous brewery. *Photo by Mike Grandmaison*

(right) Century-old limestone cottages, buildings and downtown avenues contribute to the charm of CTT's cities. *Photo by Mike Grandmaison*

Overseeing the facilitation of services across the municipal boundaries is the Regional Chair and 21 councillors who represent the citizens of the Regional Municipality of Waterloo, which, by 1999 estimates, numbered over 432,000. The Regional Council also makes policy and service decisions that affect the inhabitants of the member cities and townships.

This unified administration of services and policies, however, does not represent a diminished sense of identity for the cities and townships. On the contrary, the inhabitants of the Regional Municipality of Waterloo have relished Canadian culture, and each city and township has made some very remarkable contributions. Take, for example, ice hockey—the old Canadian standby, which typically draws an entire community together at local arenas. Indeed, some of the most impressive names in Canadian hockey history, both past and present, claim the region as their home.

Although the region has its mainstays, it has also undergone tremendous transformations in recent years. In the latter half of the twentieth century, the demographic makeup of many Ontario communities was changing, but none so rapidly as in Kitchener and Waterloo. For example, in 1976 more than 21 per cent of Kitchener's population claimed a language other than English as its mother tongue. By 1980 Germans were no longer the major participants in the Kitchener and Waterloo Regional Folk Arts Council and Multicultural Centre; the Portuguese

and Greeks, two groups which had grown greatly over three decades, formed a substantial part of the community, as did Poles, West Indians and Chinese. And so the city of Kitchener, which had long been predominantly a German experience, had become a true multicultural community.

The Regional Municipality of Waterloo has prospered greatly through the last two decades of the 20th century, and today is made up of thriving urban centres, esteemed universities, world-class manufacturers and cutting-edge technology enterprises. Perhaps its foremost attribute, however, is that the small-city, country-style experience remains; the seeds of the 21st century are well placed, but the traditions of the past still prevail. And, despite its impressive place in the global marketplace, the Region's picturesque and fertile countryside, the clean rivers and sparkling lakes, will always remain, thanks to the respectful foresight of its inhabitants. ◖◗

(left) The Regional Municipality of Waterloo is both a geographic area of Southern Ontario and an upper-tier level of municipal government, encompassing three cities and four townships in its 1,400 square kilometres. *Photo by Mike Grandmaison*

(below) Woodside National Historic Site in Kitchener is the boyhood home of former Vice President William Lyon Mackenzie King. The highlight of the site is the 14-room house, restored to the Victorian style of the 1890s. *Photo by Mike Grandmaison*

CHAPTER TWO

From Here to There 2

Building roads and super-highways, and ensuring that traffic flows within and between the area's communities, is no simple task. After all, CTT has a population of 500,000 people and is strategically positioned to serve a population of some 120 million people who live within a single day's drive. Toronto, Canada's largest city, is a mere one hour away by car. Buffalo is two hours, Windsor and Detroit three, Ottawa five and even New York City is only eight.

CTT's network of highways and roads keeps several major Canadian and U.S. cities within a day's drive. *Photo by Mike Grandmaison*

CTT's highways and roads represent a balanced approach to addressing transportation issues, making them one of the world's most modern and caring transportation systems. *Photo by Mike Grandmaison*

Canada's Technology Triangle is a prosperous, highly developed area where technology companies—to name but one sector—thrive. So where does all this balance come in? It might come in when you see all that lush farmland that seems to go on as far as the eye can see. In fact, this farmland is the richest in all of Canada so it's obvious that agriculture is very important to CTT, and not even superconductors and microchips are about to change that. But the balance also comes in when you consider the special consideration that is provided to the local Mennonites.

Just to the north are the quiet farming communities of St. Jacob's and Elmira where, for two centuries, Mennonites have lived. The Mennonites, of course, shun modern conveniences like the automobile and television, never mind the computer. The Director of Transportation's job is to reconcile all the needs of the area, and that includes the needs of these people too.

It is important to support community interests, so when the transportation department develops new bicycle routes it has to be realized that the Mennonites might not want a paved route to go by their church. That's why they are involved in the planning process. Bicycle routes are part of long-range planning since surveys show that the public wants them. Now, whenever there is a road widening, there is an effort to add separate bike lanes, and when there is a road widening in Mennonite areas extra-wide shoulders are constructed at the side for their horse-drawn buggies.

Indeed. A normal shoulder is eight feet wide, but for a Regional road like No. 86, which traverses a Mennonite community, it is 12 to 15 feet wide. Extra care must also be taken at intersections so as to accommodate the Mennonites' horses; normal curbs are six inches high, but in areas frequented by the horses the curbs are smoothed out so as not to cause injury. Needless to say, this is a balanced approach to a modern and caring transportation system.

It is said in real estate that the secret is "location, location, location." The same adage could easily apply to CTT. While managing to preserve both valuable farmland and traditional ways of life, the area has opened its arms to the modern age. CTT's location, which is one of its most cherished attributes, has a lot to do with that.

The area is extremely well connected—by highway, rail and air—to not only key markets in North America, but the whole world. The global marketplace. And that includes the information highway as well since the telecommunications infrastructure in CTT matches or surpasses that of most major business and financial centres.

First of all, there is ready access to Highway 401, which is easily Canada's busiest. It runs right through the centre of CTT so virtually no one in Cambridge, Guelph, Kitchener or Waterloo is more than a few minutes away. The 401 runs west to Windsor and Detroit, and east to Toronto and points east of that metropolis; in fact, all the way to the province of Quebec. For the portion of the 401 that is within CTT's domain, the road is a six-lane divided highway, which is important for an economy where major manufacturing concerns rely heavily on "just-in-time."

Toyota, which locates its Canadian head office as well as a major manufacturing facility on Fountain Street in Cambridge, maintains only a two-hour inventory on site at all times. Of course, a big plus for CTT business and industry is that the area is virtually free of traffic jams, which makes it unique.

Within CTT itself, an excellent highway system allows for efficient movement of people and goods among the local communities. Conestoga Parkway, which was built in the late 1960s, is a four-lane divided highway and is being developed further; the Ontario Ministry of Transportation and Communications deemed it important enough for a

$50-million project that will see a new three-level interchange installed at Conestoga and Highway 8. Highway 8 itself runs north from the 401 to serve Kitchener-Waterloo while Franklin Boulevard is a four-lane arterial road that runs through the heart of Cambridge. Another important artery in CTT is Highway 6. From a point 17 kilometers east of Highway 8, it runs north from the 401 to Guelph while Highway 6 southbound, running to Hamilton, is another four kilometers to the east.

Thus, the local highway and arterial road system constitutes a first-class feeder system that effectively serves every need from the family outing to trucking delivery schedules. The modern industrial parks in CTT are also well connected by road. Rounding out the highway system is nearby access to the new electronic toll route—Highway 407—which runs north of Toronto and has become a prime alternate to the 401. It, along with the long-established Highway 7, also provides excellent access to CTT.

Tremendous access to Toronto in particular is a great benefit to a lot of people here. Thousands of people locate in CTT because of proximity to Toronto. For example, a new residential development is going into Cambridge and

A great deal of care is taken when roads traverse Mennonite communities; highway shoulders in such areas range from 12 to 15 feet wide to accommodate horse-drawn carriages.
Photo by Mike Grandmaison

Agri-business, the study of business and technologies relevant to agriculture, is of key importance in shaping the destiny of CTT's educational
system, agricultural institutions, and economy.
Photo by Mike Grandmaison

The University of Guelph has carved an impressive niche the science and business of agriculture. With the city of Guelph's substantial reputation in this field, the local university has come to play a major role in the study of agri-business. *Photo by Mike Grandmaison*

places about 1,000 students a year in business and other areas on its placement program. Students from the business faculty are usually finalists in almost every national and international business competition they enter. Recent successes include first place in Canada and second internationally at the MT&T Dalhousie International Business Case Competition. The school's market niche also includes social work, music and accounting, so it's no surprise that Laurier students have won the prestigious Gunn Award as the top accounting students in all of Canada—and not only once, but two years running.

Along with UW and Guelph, Laurier has strong ties to the business community of CTT. PRISM is a student-fund-

ed and student-managed organization in Laurier's business school that offers the latest in information technology and information technology training. Another organization called STEP—with concerns in biology, chemistry, physics and computing and psychology—funds everything from lectures and equipment purchases to student research in all these respective fields. Laurier has also joined forces with the other two universities in CTT to develop a tri-university automated library system that benefits students and faculty alike.

Rounding out the impressive post-secondary environment in CTT is Conestoga College, one of the 25 community colleges in Ontario. Conestoga's total enrollment including full-time, diploma, certificate, part-time and continuing education students is more than 31,000. The largest campus is the Doon campus in Kitchener, which includes a Recreation Centre, Early Childhood Education Centre, Automated Technology Training Centre and Woodworking Centre of Ontario. The latter is a 58,000-square-foot training facility for Ontario's secondary wood products processing industry. The Automated Technology Training Centre, meanwhile, specializes in electrical, control technology, maintenance technology and robotics and automation.

But none of CTT's four post-secondary institutions would even exist if not for the younger students, and that's where the public school and separate school boards come into play. Waterloo Region District School Board is one of the largest in Ontario, providing public education for seven municipalities in Waterloo Region. Serving almost 60,000 students in 100 elementary schools and 15 secondary schools, it is also very active in continuing education programs and adult learning courses. In addition, about 2,000 local businesses are involved in co-operative education with the board. Along with regular day programs, full-time adult education, continuing education and summer school, the board offers core French and French immersion, special education, international language programs and language instruction for new Canadians.

The publicly-funded Waterloo Catholic District School Board involves 46 elementary schools, five secondary schools, and three adult education schools. The adult schools are quite unique, with courses encompassing everything from English language to mathematics for business and for technology to parenting, accounting and various computer offerings.

The philosophy, indeed the very culture of CTT, involves ongoing education and lifelong learning with strong ties to the community. The roots were simple and the road has been a long one, but the rewards have been tremendous.

When Abraham Erb built a log schoolhouse around his mills on Beaver Creek in 1820, all who lived in the small village soon to be named Waterloo were very happy. After all, the building was a dedicated school. It was a big improvement over the existing makeshift school that had occupied only part of a little log house on the south side of Mill Street. But anything that grows has to start small. The unparalleled educational community of CTT today

has indeed come a long way from those early origins. The nice thing about it is that people here don't forget. [■◄

Collegiate athletic games are a common sight in CTT, an area enriched by the presence of three universities and one community college. *Photo by Mike Grandmaison*

UNIVERSITY OF WATERLOO

The University of Waterloo is one of Canada's most successful and prestigious universities, a destination of choice for the country's top students and an attractive place for professors to establish careers in teaching and research. UW currently enrolls 15,500 full-time undergraduates and 1500 graduate students. With the world's largest co-operative education (work-study) program, Waterloo boasts active links with some 2,600 businesses, industries and agencies across Canada and around the world.

UW's student body can choose co-op or take the regular system of study (non co-op), and 109 program options in six faculties and four university colleges. And, with its 44 post-baccalaureate programs, 28 at the doctoral level, UW has become one of the country's leading centres for graduate studies, attracting exemplary students who annually win more than their share of research awards.

Research, innovation, teaching excellence, high academic standards, community involvement. Small wonder the University of Waterloo has been described "by a clear margin, the most successful of all universities created in Canada in the last 50 years." - Sir John Daniel, Vice-Chancellor of the Open University, U.K.

CHAPTER FOUR

An Extraordinary Quality of Life

4

Any community that values education the way CTT does is naturally going to place a lot of emphasis on the care of its inhabitants. CTT which encompasses a veritable community of cities, towns, villages and hamlets is just as much a leader in health care, social services and conservation as it is in postsecondary learning. But this isn't surprising. After all, investing in its people has been a hallmark of this region since the first Europeans arrived two centuries ago.

Clean, manicured parks allow CTT residents the opportunity to enjoy relaxing, exercising and playing outdoors. *Photo by Mike Grandmaison*

The presence of recycling facilities such as this oil recovery plant near the Waterloo airport is one representation of CTT's efforts to preserve and protect the earth's natural resources. *Photo by Mike Grandmaison*

This philosophy of caring goes back to the land. Because of the proud agrarian roots of the area, taking care of the land and its people has long been the prime concern. For the first half century of its existence, Waterloo County was largely rural. The county government supported agriculture through grants to agricultural fairs and rural organizations, and even established the appointment of a "county pupil" to the Ontario Agricultural College. In the 20th century, as the towns got bigger and the notion of urbanization had to coexist with the traditional rural roots, conservation of the land became paramount. It was seen in the form of effective woodlot management and various projects to maintain water tables, prevent erosion and preserve the natural beauty of forests and woodlands. Then, in the 1940s, the county started purchasing acreages for reforestation purposes. In the 1960s the Ontario Ministry of Lands and Forests got involved as the manager of forest lands, and new legislation like the Trees Act and Forestry Act ensured the continued preservation of valuable wildlife habitats, not to mention flood and erosion protection and water supplies. Indeed, all of these concerns were part of the raison d'étre behind the formation of the new Regional Municipality of Waterloo in the early 1970s.

As the population continued to grow and the area prospered, the principle of solid waste management was a growing concern. In 1973 the region assumed control of all the landfill sites that had been operated by local municipalities. Modern environmental controls were established at landfill sites and waste transfer facilities, and in 1991 the Materials Recycling Centre at the Waterloo Landfill Site was opened. Likewise, the city of Guelph today has one of the most evolved recycling programs in the world and is considered one of the most environmentally responsible cities in North America. This accolade can be attributed to its 3,000-household and soon-to-be citywide recycling program and wet/dry recycling facility. In fact, Guelph's wet/dry recycling establishment is recognized as the foremost facility of its kind—not just in Ontario and across Canada, but in the entire world.

This philosophy of caring for the land had embraced a new version of the three R's: reduce, reuse, recycle.

And the people, of course, were never forgotten.

Just as CTT cares for its land and its many valuable natural resources, so too does it cherish that most important resource of all—those who live and work in the region. Today CTT provides nothing less than world-class health care. As a matter of fact, the health care providers in CTT—including leading hospitals and institutions specializing in emergency and preventative care—are among the best in Canada. The reorganization of health care in Ontario during the 1990s resulted in some extensive hospital redevelopment in CTT. Guelph General Hospital was renovated and expanded so it could serve as the acute care hospital for the city. This meant 135,000 square feet of new construction added to the existing 205,000-square-foot facility, and the addition of state-of-the-art technologies.

Guelph General Hospital opened its doors in 1875 with 12 beds, a small infectious room and a dispensary. A superintendent and two nurses provided care. But times have changed. The Hospital Redevelopment Project in Guelph, scheduled to end in the year 2000, will result in the integration of all acute care services, including those previously provided by Guelph General Hospital and St. Joseph's Hospital & Home. The move effectively relocates all services on the one hospital site. The institution's comprehensive, acute-care facility now provides 24-hour emergency coverage, advanced technology and diagnostic support and specialty programs such as orthopedics, cardiac care, obstetrics, gynecology and pediatrics.

Also in Guelph is the privately owned Homewood Health Centre, which offers treatments for mental illness and behavioural disorders for patients who come from across Canada and even from overseas. A mere one-hour drive west of Toronto, this 300-bed facility is located on 50 scenic acres and has developed an international reputation as a top provider in mental and behavioural health care.

The single largest medical institution in CTT is Grand River Hospital, also known as the Kitchener-Waterloo Health Centre. The sole provider of pediatric care for the communities of Kitchener, Waterloo and surrounding

Clean-up efforts launched by volunteer groups help keep CTT's land and water clean and safe. *Photo by B. Joan Barber*

Guelph's wet/dry recycling facility is recognized as one of the finest examples in the world. *Photo by Mike Grandmaison*

St. Mary's General Hospital in Kitchener was the second hospital in North America to automatically download vital signs from a computerized monitoring system to its MEDITECH computers in the critical care unit and recovery rooms. *Photo courtesy of St. Mary's General Hospital*

townships, it is Ontario's second largest birthing centre with some 4,000 births a year. It's no surprise then that the Parent and Children's Program offers leading neonatal, obstetrical and pediatric care. The hospital's Childbirth Services offers family-centred support from early pregnancy to one-month post delivery; services include a prebirth clinic, screening for potential at-risk or high-risk pregnancies and a Special Care Nursery where infants with moderate to potential high-risk problems are cared for by a special team of professionals.

In addition, the hospital's Children's Services unit provides both inpatient and outpatient care, the latter including clinics for Cystic Fibrosis, Juvenile Diabetes Education, Pediatric Oncology and General Pediatrics. The Kitchener-Waterloo Health Centre also works closely with other community agencies such as the Waterloo Region Community Department and the Community Care Access Centre. They all share the same objective: to better prepare families for dealing with pregnancy, birth

First-rate public and private hospitals ensure
CTT residents the finest in health care. Pictured
above is Riverslea Homewood Hospital in
Guelph, recognized worldwide for its treatment
of mental illness and behavioural disorders.
Photo by B. Norm Jary

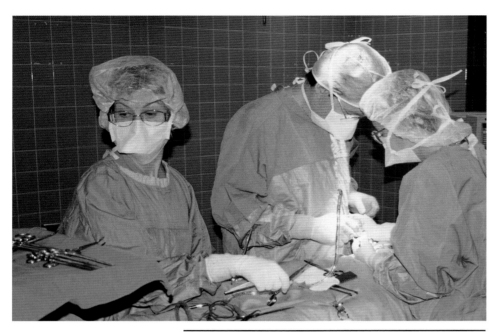

Founded in 1924 by the Sisters of St. Joseph of Hamilton, St. Mary's General Hospital is today part of St. Joseph's Health Care System. *Photo courtesy of St. Mary's Hospital.*

and what's involved in caring for a new infant. On the horizon for this major health care centre is a full-service Regional Cancer Treatment Centre, a Magnetic Resonance Imaging (MRI) unit and establishment of longer-term mental health services.

Another important health care institution in Kitchener is St. Mary's General Hospital. Founded in 1924 by the Sisters of St. Joseph of Hamilton, it is part of St. Joseph's Health Care System. This system encompasses institutions in CTT and beyond with a common goal of sharing expertise, boosting efficiency and reducing costs. It was the second hospital in North America to automatically download vital signs from a computerized monitoring system to its MEDITECH computer system in the critical care unit and recovery rooms. This system naturally saves nurses a lot of valuable time. St. Mary's also rates as the quickest-response health care institution in Ontario for delivering emergency cardiac treatment. In 1997 it became the emergency orthopedic hospital for the north Waterloo Region, specializing in everything from hip fractures to multiple injuries and trauma.

In Cambridge, Cambridge Memorial Hospital is the health care institution of record with its many core and specialty programs. It has been around since 1888 when it was known as Galt Hospital. Today its core programs include oncology, palliative care, medicine, family and child health, critical care and surgery. Specialty programs include an Ambulatory Care Centre that hosts outpatient rehabilitation, as well as a day hospital, wellness centre, community mental health clinic, diabetes education program and psychogeriatric clinic. Cambridge Memorial

Medical research and the development of medical technology in CTT's hospitals helps to increase the quality of life for people throughout the world through the dissemination of important medical innovations. *Photo courtesy of the University of Guelph.*

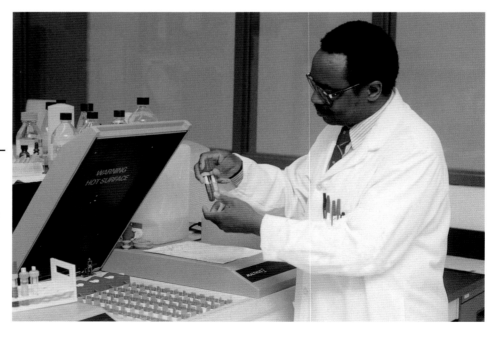

CTT visitors and residents can watch over 1000 animals live and play in a natural setting at the Africa Lion Safari in Cambridge. The animals, representing over 100 species indigenous to Africa and other continents, include elephants, giraffes, zebras, and of course, lions. *Photos by Mike Grandmaison*

Photo by Mike Grandmaison

In Flanders Fields

*In Flanders fields the poppies blow
Between the crosses, row on row,
That mark our place; and in the sky
The larks, still bravely singing, fly
Scarce heard amidst the guns below.*

*We are the Dead. Short days ago
We lived, felt dawn, saw sunset glow,
Loved, and were loved, and now we lie
In Flanders fields.*

*Take up our quarrel with the foe:
To you from failing hands we throw
The torch; be yours to hold it high.
If ye break faith with us who die
We shall not sleep, though poppies grow
In Flanders fields.*

all about. Built in 1858, the charming limestone cottage was the home of David and Janet McCrae, but it's their son, Colonel John McCrae, to whom the house is dedicated. A noted doctor, soldier, author and artist, Colonel McCrae distinguished himself in World War I when treating the wounded during the Second Battle of Ypres in 1915. After presiding at the burial service of a close friend, he was compelled to write "In Flanders Fields":

Built in 1858, this lime-stone cottage was the home of Colonel John McCrae, a noted doctor, soldier, author and artist, who, after presiding at the burial service of a close friend, was compelled to write "In Flanders Fields." *Photo by Mike Grandmaison*

Early eveing sun casts a warm glow on the Church of Our Lady Immaculate in Guelph. *Photo by Mike Grandmaison*

The poem has been forever linked to Canada's role in both World Wars, and because of that legacy, the McCrae House remains a major attraction that tugs at the heartstrings and very soul of the people. The room settings depict the daily life of a young, middle-class Guelph family, and a permanent exhibition gallery tells the story of Colonel McCrae, who died in 1918 after contracting pneumonia while in France. His renowned poem, however, lives on amidst the beautiful gardens and memorial park around the house. Indeed, it lives on in the souls of war veterans everywhere and in the souls of Canadians who were born long after John McCrae died. This is the kind of thing that's typical of the people of Cambridge, Guelph, Kitchener, Waterloo and the Regional Municipality of Waterloo. It is typical of a people who cherish what they have and who haven't forgotten just what it took to get there. [■]

A wedding party gathers in Cambridge's Soper Park, not an uncommon site in summer when CTT residents take to the outdoors to enjoy the warm temperatures. *Photo by Mike Grandmaison*

(above) Illustrative of CTT's social diversity, largely agrarian and non-technical people, such as the Mennonite boy above, live within minutes of the some of the most technologically adept institutions in the world. *Photo by Mike Grandmaison*

(opposite) A summer street market in Guelph attracts vendors and shoppers from all over CTT. *Photo by E. Barber*

CHAPTER SIX

From Farming to Fibre Optics

6

When Richard Cater of Leroux Steel was asked why the Quebec-based distributor of carbon steel products selected Canada's Technology Triangle as the site of its latest distribution centre, it didn't take him long to answer. "Location," he said. The company, which has distribution centres throughout eastern Canada and the United States, had purchased a 20-acre site in Cambridge for a 160,000-square-foot storage facility; the new distribution centre opened in January, 1999, employing 100 people.

The economy of CTT forms a diverse and dynamic society—a place where people from all walks of life can live and work.
Photo by Mike Grandmaison

Photo by Mike Grandmaison

"This area is central," said Cater, who is Vice President of Business Development for Leroux Steel. "We're two hours from Windsor, an hour and a half from Toronto, six from Montreal and three from Buffalo. We are within a 500-mile radius of 150 million people and we're just a two-minute drive to the 401 highway. We also have the benefit of a diversified economy and a diversified labour force. Really you can't beat it."

You can't. CTT is one of the fastest growing economic areas in Canada. Indeed, as the area's industrial base has expanded in recent years, CTT is no longer one of those proverbial "best-kept secrets." Today it boasts more than 14,000 businesses which reach out to a great many sectors. The manufacturing sector itself is widely diversified and the service sector is large and able.

Growth is often easy to measure, and in CTT the rate of growth has been nothing short of spectacular. In a four-year time frame—1993 through 1997—the number of computing services in CTT grew by more than 50 per cent. During the same period, the number of engineering consulting firms grew by 38 per cent, management consulting firms by 35 per cent and other scientific and technical services by over 40 per cent. Most of this growth was from smaller firms, which should come as no surprise since small business is the biggest growth area in business today.

Leading the pack of these new enterprises were business services companies, followed by trades contracting, health and social services, food and beverage and automobile sales and service. In fact, from 1985 to 1995, the total number of unincorporated businesses in CTT rose by 72 per cent. But CTT has its share of large companies too, some of them going back many years. Those firms employing over 1,000 people include the likes of J. M. Schneider Inc. (manufacturer of processed meats, poultry, cheese, bakery goods), Linamar Corporation (maker of machines and assembled automotive components), Babcock & Wilcox (manufacturer of steam-generating systems and services), Kaufman Footwear, Toyota Motor Manufacturing Canada Inc. and Uniroyal Goodrich Tire Manufacturing.

A profile of CTT's top ten industry sectors holds few surprises for an area that has quickly emerged as one of the

world's leading high-tech engines. The computer industry is solidly ensconced in the top ten sectors, including environmental, manufacturing, test & measurement, biotechnology, industrial automation, telecommunications, photonics, energy and medical technologies.

Location and diversification aside, a major attribute of CTT is its well-educated, highly trained labour force—at last count about a quarter of a million strong. Choose any indicator you want—participation rate, education level, etc.—and consistently it comes out on top. The four post-secondary educational institutions in the area contribute greatly to the economy, providing a steady stream of new graduates to meet the demanding needs of industry and business. As a matter of fact, many of Canada's brightest and best young people have chosen CTT as the place to begin their careers.

Probably the biggest key to making it happen within CTT is the teamwork that exists among business, education and government. The municipalities that comprise CTT—Cambridge, Guelph, Kitchener, Waterloo and the Regional Municipality of Waterloo—all actively promote the development of a business-friendly environment. While economic diversity is the order of the day for CTT with healthy vibrant sectors in the automotive, high-tech, manufacturing, insurance, and financial services industries, each of the municipalities has its own unique strengths. Cambridge and Kitchener are both centres of manufacturing excellence. Guelph wields an international reputation in agriculture / agri-business. And, Waterloo's impression on the high-tech world is one of the largest and most significant anywhere.

All the municipalities, in fact, certainly realize the importance of maintaining business-friendly environments. This is in ample evidence with the many modern business parks in CTT. Cambridge has three of them: Cambridge Business Park, located near the 400-acre Toyota plant; the 1,200-acre L. G. Lovell park; and Eastern Industrial Park in the city's interior. Guelph has the city-owned Hanlon Business Park and York-Watson Industrial Park, the privately owned Northwood Business

Guelph's role in CTT and its ties to the global marketplace have sustained not just a community of successful technology institutions, but a broad range of service industries. The same also holds true for the other key CTT cities. *Photo by Mike Grandmaison*

CALDWELL

In 1990, having already accumulated a large, influential clientele over a stellar 20-year career, Robert Caldwell decided to form his own company and he embarked on a strategic course that had never yet been attempted in Canada. He pioneered what became known as the Correspondent Network—a group of independently owned brokerage firms.

Today, a growing list of companies is looking to Robert Caldwell Capital Corporation and Caldwell Investment Banking Inc. for the financial assistance to help accommodate both their retail brokerage and corporate financial requirements. Whether an individual or firm requires a single financial product or new capital to support corporate growth plans, the Caldwell group will deliver, thanks to a wide range of services that includes retail brokerage, mergers and acquisitions, equity financing and venture capital.

Since its inception, the Robert Caldwell Capital Corporation and Caldwell Investment Banking Inc. has formed a strong reputation for its intimate connection with the economic growth of Canada's Technology Triangle. Widely reputed as a company plugged in to the community's growth, investors from across North America beat a steady path to the Caldwell group's door in their search for new investment opportunities.

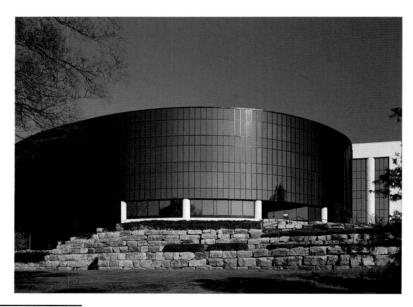

The rise of business parks and new office buildings testifies to CTT's economic growth.
Photo by Mike Grandmaison

Park and the University of Guelph's Research Park. Kitchener, meanwhile, has over 500 acres of land available for industrial and commercial development, and 70 of these acres sit in municipal business parks, such as Lancaster Corporate Centre near the Conestoga Expressway and Huron Business Park, with its aesthetically-designed locations for manufacturing and service businesses. Finally, Waterloo has Northland Business Park and Eastbridge Business Park.

Certainly one of the going concerns in CTT is Communitech. CTT's community technology association, Communitech is a partnership that brings together technology companies, technology service companies, educational institutions and all levels of government. They all operate together to create a true world-class technology business centre. Communitech's activities include networking sessions, business exchange seminars and strong community initiatives designed to expand technology growth. As the voice of CTT's technology industry, this organization has over 140 members working to realize the goals of strengthening the current CTT technology companies while attracting new technology companies to the area, providing a business climate conducive to technology start-ups and fostering an environment to attract and keep employees in CTT.

"We compete with Silicon Valley in California, Route 128 in Boston, the Ottawa region and anywhere that focuses on high technology," says Vince Schiralli, President of Communitech. "We all work together—the mayors, the economic development offices, the chief administrative officers. I just love the job since I get to spend time with the movers and shakers of the high-tech industry, and many of these people are really brilliant."

Ninety-five per cent of the technology companies in CTT conduct business outside of Canada. They are

exporters. Many of the newer firms are spin-offs from the academic world, especially from the University of Waterloo, which has an international reputation for its high-tech excellence. Some sources estimate that the university has spun off some 400 companies over the years, and it is for that reason that some regard UW as the patriarch of a large family tree.

Tradition and aesthetics have not been lost to modernization, new development and the onward push of progress in CTT. *Photo by Mike Grandmaison*

Guelph has experienced some of the fastest economic growth in Ontario, making it one of the nation's most interesting and dynamic cities. *Photo by Mike Grandmaison*

(below) Waterloo's impression on the high-tech world is one of the largest and most significant anywhere. *Photo by Mike Grandmaison*

Harnessing the power of light to cut through metals and other materials at Vantage Laser Cutting, Limited's facilities—just one example of the application of high technology in CTT industry.
Photo by Mike Grandmaison

There's little surprise that agri-business has become so important to CTT. The region not only has some of the most productive farmland in Canada, it is home to cities and institutions regarded worldwide as hotbeds of technology. *Photo by Mike Grandmaison*

One of the more notable UW graduates is Randal Howard who earned his degree in Honours Mathematics and Computer Science back in 1975. Nine years later he founded his own company, MKS Inc., a business-to-business software provider. Today MKS has 210 employees, creates $35 million in revenues and is active around the world. Howard is a founding member of both Communitech and The Atlas Group, a CEO forum for high-tech companies in CTT.

"The Atlas Group is for peer mentoring while Communitech is a focused organization with a paid staff," Howard says. "The mandate is to make CTT one of the most advanced technology centres in the world and it already is the fastest-growing one in Canada. We're competitive on a world scale. My own company doesn't exist as an island and there are lots of things a company can't do by itself. This is where an organization like Communitech comes in handy."

Howard says CTT's high-tech sector can expect a growth rate of more than 30 per cent per year in employee headcount, and even more than that in terms of revenues and exports. "It's a pretty compelling picture," he says.

A vital cog in CTT's business community is CTTAN, a community-based initiative designed to accelerate the growth and commercial success of local growth-oriented companies. CTTAN, with a board comprised of eight business leaders and aligned with Communitech, facilitates the placement of risk capital into new firms.

Another key player in CTT's technology community is the Ontario Centre for Environmental Technology Advancement (OCETA). It is a private-sector, not-for-profit corporation dedicated to helping small- and medium-sized companies develop and market new environmental technologies. OCETA's knowledge of the environment industry in Ontario stems from experience with over 500 clients whose products and services represent everything from water treatment to waste management, energy efficiency and recycling.

Much of the success of CTT is due to the spirit of cooperation that exists between the business sector and the educational community. A good example of this cooperation is the Research Centre for Management of New Technology (REMAT), which helps the private sector take advantage of the resources of the Wilfrid Laurier University School of Business and Economics; REMAT

Immersed in entrepreneurial ventures and technological innovation, CTT offers a business climate that is ideal for networking, partnership and growth. *Photo by Martin Schwalbe.*

helps companies acquire and implement new technology in the workplace. It also provides guidance in management training in a technology-driven environment. Likewise, the University of Guelph offers assistance to business and industry through a group called CR&D (Collaborative Research and Development). CR&D coordinates the university's activities and policies with industrial contract research, technology transfer and the commercialization of technology.

The Laurier Trade Development Centre (LTDC) helps small- and medium-sized companies become more globally competitive. The LTDC researches trade issues around the world and even has an office in Mexico City where it has developed an expertise in business development with Mexico. The LTDC is recognized as a leader in Mexican and NAFTA (North American Free Trade Agreement) business development circles.

Rick Thompson is executive director of CTT and he's keenly aware of the importance of global marketing. In 1997 he not only became the organization's very first employee, but he also went on a major trade mission to Latin America. He was one of 400 Canadian business leaders on the trip which included Canadian Prime Minister Jean Chretien.

"We spent 15 days in Mexico, Brazil, Argentina and Chile," Thompson says. "It was a great opportunity to meet with leaders from Canadian business and to make contacts. There are a great many companies in CTT doing business around the world today so this kind of exposure and learning is important. We all try to work together to make it happen."

However, while Thompson is quick to promote the technology smarts of CTT, he also points out that the area offers more than just technology. Indeed, the traditional business roots of CTT are in a very different area—agriculture.

Back in the middle of the 19th century, wheat was easily the dominant crop of farmers' fields in Waterloo County and it was, for the time, big business. The local

Cambridge is home to Automation Tooling Systems, one of the world's largest producers of custom-designed factory automation systems. *Photos courtesy of ATS.*

The Guelph-based Semex Alliance is regarded as the world leader in the bovine breeding industry and is widely recognized for its powerful Holstein cows with superior characteristics and outstanding milk producing capabilities. *Photo by Mike Grandmaison*

farmers seldom specialized. Their crops included beans, buckwheat, turnips, hay, flax seed and potatoes, in addition to apples and maple sugar. This, of course, was all in addition to a thriving trade in dairy products. It wasn't long before oats surpassed wheat production. Whatever the crops, farms of this area were among the most productive in Canada and have remained so to this day, but now CTT can reap the benefits of agriculture combined with technology.

The word making the rounds today is agri-business. Larry Milligan, vice president of research at the University of Guelph and as close to a visionary in this field as there is, explains that a bona fide agri-food sector has emerged in and around Guelph.

"You can call it 'agri-business' but a more accurate term is food system business," Milligan says. "KPMG did an evaluation of economic turnover in the Ontario food business sector and concluded that it's worth $63 billion a year. This involves things like production of food products, food processing and transportation, and it's largely focused around this area. We think we can build a big advantage in international competitiveness with an emphasis on high quality here."

Exemplifying just how significant the food business is— not just to the immediate region and Ontario, but to all of Canada—is the Agri-Food Quality Cluster based in Guelph. A support structure comprised of technology institutions, universities, government divisions, agricultural

Agri-business and the agri-food sector
centered in Guelph have helped improve
crop diversity, quality and yield throughout
CTT. *Photos by Mike Grandmaison*

The importance of agri-business and the agri-food industry to the region has all but guaranteed that CTT's bustling cities will always be tempered with quiet, bucolic land-scapes. *Photo by Mike Grandmaison*

industries and private sectors, the Agri-Food Quality Cluster combines the strengths of each to maintain and manage the $63-billion dollar agri-food industry in Ontario. It's a tremendous task, considering that the agri-food industry, which encompasses on-farm inputs, production, food and beverage processing, food service, retail food sales and exports, is second in size only to the auto industry in Ontario. In fact, more than half the nation's food and beverage processing industry is located in southern Ontario and 640,00 people are employed in the industry.

According to Milligan, "Guelph has been to the agri-food business what Waterloo has been to computer technology. The food business is becoming much different. Now there is a systems approach to yielding products and services. In the future, you will see a lot of new business starts by graduates of the University of Guelph, and more and more multinationals having operations around here. I think it's safe to say that Guelph is going to be a magnet. But that's true of the whole CTT." [◾]

Photo by Mike Grandmaison

Photo by Mike Grandmaison

Photo by Mike Grandmaison

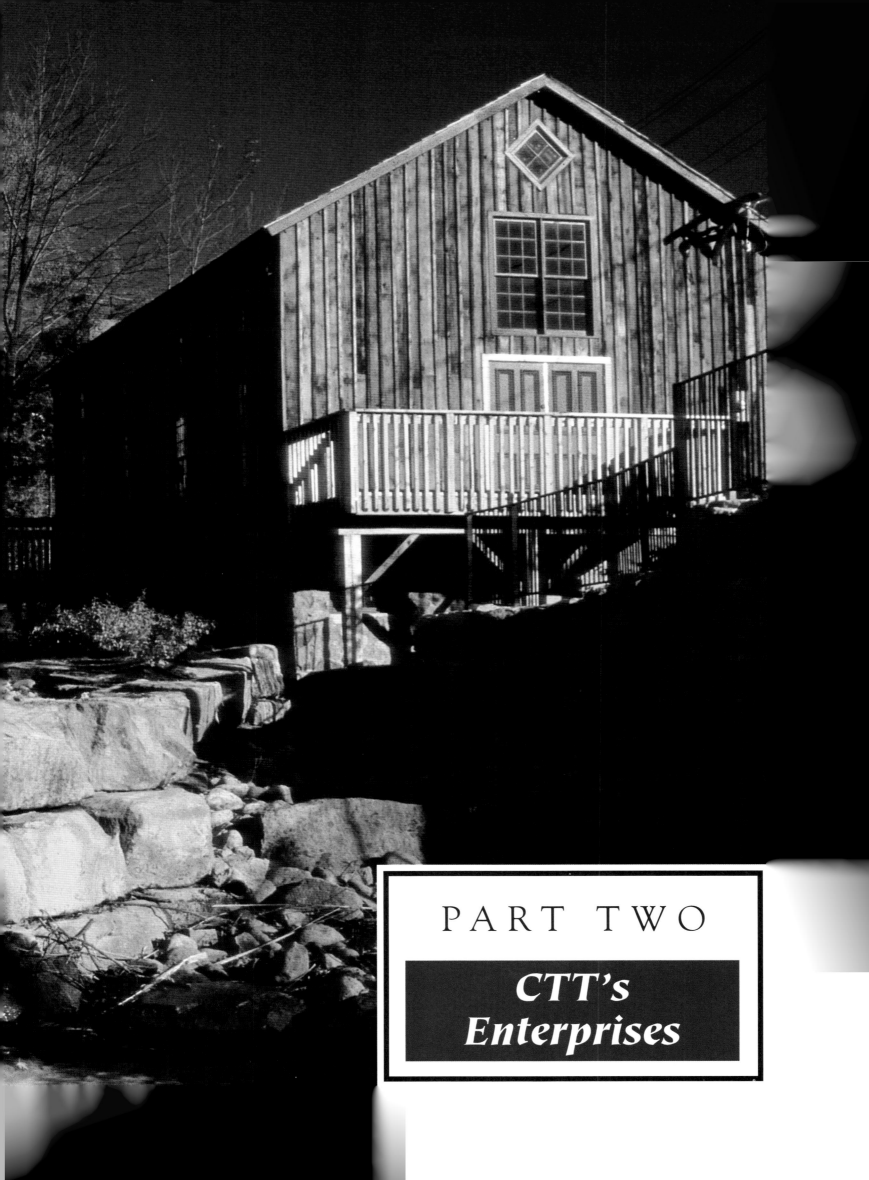

PART TWO

CTT's Enterprises

CHAPTER SEVEN

Leadership

7

. Photo by Mike Grandmaison

Anyone who doubts Mill Creek Motor Freight's standards for excellence should perhaps visit the company's Cambridge headquarters.

There, amid a constant din of employee activity, visitors would come across a large wall aglitter with plaques, trophies and mementos of appreciation.

And someone like Bob Simpson, Mill Creek's vice-president of Sales and Marketing, would be only too glad to point out some of the particular awards. He'd probably highlight the Purolator Courier of the Year award for excellence in ground transportation, which Mill Creek has won two years in a row. He'd likely refer to the Xerox Canada Supplier of the Year plaque or the Provincial Transportation Ministry's Ontario Gold Award of Excellence.

He might also regale the visitor with the story of a 20-year-old company that continues to grow thanks to its genuine dedication to customer service, not to mention its proactive environmental and community contributions.

Mill Creek Motor Freight was founded in 1978 in a tiny facility that housed three trucks. Its founder and president, the Cambridge-born-and-raised Phil Henning, decided his trucking firm would zero in on the high-value, sensitive freight market by offering both specialized equipment and handling.

The company, now some 575 employees strong, has never looked back. By the early 1980s, Mill Creek outgrew its original headquarters and moved to another area of the city. Today, the company boasts 300 trucks. Its full-service headquarters, already 20 times larger than Mill Creek's original home, is about to undergo another massive expansion to accommodate unabated, but strategic, growth.

And recently, Alberta's Mullen Transportation Inc. (MTI), a publicly-traded company which provides management and financial expertise, technology and systems support to its subsidiaries, purchased 100 per cent interest in Mill Creek. MTI manages a network of carrier companies across the country and is one of the largest providers of trucking and logistics services in Canada, with a fleet of more than 800 trucks and 1,500 trailers, many of them specialized.

The companies now form an alliance to jointly market their trucking and logistic service throughout North America. They will also share facilities and equipment and, consistent with their respective reputations, continue to benchmark best practices in all areas of the business.

And in making the announcement of the purchase, MTI President and CEO Murray Mullen cited Mill Creek as "one of Canada's premier air-ride logistic van carriers."

Certainly, the company has earned that reputation. Its formidable fleet transports everything from electronics to high-value furniture throughout North America and Mexico. In 1990, the company opened a terminal in Holland, Michigan, to help streamline deliveries throughout the United States. To expedite freight in and out of Mexico, it opened a terminal in Laredo, Texas. And to provide expedited, overnight deliveries throughout Ontario and Quebec, the company acquired an LTL carrier named Jett Linehaul.

And most of this growth has been achieved without the benefit of a direct sales force. Mill Creek is a company whose ongoing expansion is directly linked to its glowing reputation.

At Mill Creek, its extensively trained, highly motivated drivers are regarded as the company's unofficial sales force. Each new driver here undergoes an exhaustive orientation in which customer service expectations are stressed, and detailed, hands-on instruction in all aspects of special freight handling is provided.

Consequently, the company's claims and damage-to-freight rate, as well as its safety record, rank among the best in the industry. Furthermore, the company is highly proactive in ensuring that deliveries are problem free. Its representatives make direct contact, for instance, with everyone in the chain, from the shipper to the ultimate consignee, so that everyone understands the process. Should a problem occur, Mill Creek

immediately enlightens the consignee. The bottom line is no unpleasant surprises or, as a company pamphlet suggests, "no headaches" for customers.

So it's not surprising that Mill Creek Motor Freight boasts many major, long-term customers, including IBM, Xerox Canada, Canadian General Tower and Rockwell Automation. Or that the vast majority of its new business is the direct result of referrals from existing clientele.

But although Mill Creek drivers provide the front-line manifestation of the company's dedication to customer service, it continues to implement countless behind-the-scenes changes to maximize its ability to both serve its clientele, and keep pace with the ever-changing realities of the trucking industry.

All of its trucks, of course, are air-ride and come specially equipped to handle the most sensitive of loads. However, in recognition of an industry where the fast, efficient exchange of information has become increasingly crucial, Mill Creek has also developed every technical tool available.

Among other things, the company has kept pace with the advancing technology by introducing EDI capabilities for its clients and computerizing its dispatch operations. Today, Mill Creek drivers can send and receive messages using on-board laptop terminals via a small satellite antenna, and its central dispatch can monitor the location of any of the company's trucks and shipments almost instantly.

But at Mill Creek, that's still not enough. The company's search for further enhancements in the communication process never really stops. And so in 1999, Mill Creek introduced a system allowing customers direct access to their dispatched system, via the Internet.

Meanwhile, Mill Creek continues to keep abreast of developments in the trucking industry through its active involvement with such organizations as the Ontario Trucking Association and the Canadian Trucking Alliance. It also keeps up to date on world-class business fundamentals through its affiliation with the High Performance Manufacturing Consortium (HPM). The HPM membership, which includes General Electric Multilin, Velcro Canada,

Cami Automotive and Steelcase to name a few, work together to enable each new member to optimize their competitiveness in a win-win environment using shared resources and experience.

In October 1998, Mill Creek received the QMI ISO 9002 certification, supporting their quality initiatives. Process improvements have been implemented that directly impact overall customer service.

Mill Creek's prosperity hasn't come at the expense of the environment, either. In fact, a nationally distributed newsletter published by Canada's Ministry of Natural Resources recently featured the company as an example of the hand-in-hand partnership prosperity can forge with environmental concern.

"The company," states this particular article, "constantly monitors vehicle specifications and performance and implements changes to improve safety, efficiency and emissions."

Within the last two years, for example, Mill Creek reduced its average vehicle weight by more than 450 kilograms (1,000 pounds) by using ultra-light aluminum components.

Some of Cambridge's community institutions and agencies could also cite Mill Creek as an example of prosperity working hand-in-hand with community involvement and generosity. Because Mill Creek Motor Freight, whose list of community causes includes Cambridge Memorial Hospital, and Conestoga College, believes its role as a corporate citizen goes beyond the provision of employment opportunities.

Indeed, on that aforementioned, award-bedecked wall is a shiny plaque presented by the area's United Way agency. It's called the Chairman's Award, and it is given annually to the company boasting the highest per-capita contribution.

"It's fundamentally a personal choice," Bob Simpson says of Mill Creek Motor Freight's reputation for generosity. "You have to remember we're all from this area. We love this community, and feel a responsibility to give something back to it." [■]

(top) Maclean's Magazine calls Waterloo Canada's "best overall" universities in its annual reputational survey.

(bottom) Waterloo offers undergraduate and graduate programs in Arts, Applied Health Sciences, Engineering, Environmental Studies, Mathematics and Science.

For the record, the naysayers have long since been proven wrong. Today, 42 years later, UW's co-op program encompasses over 9,000 of the school's 16,000 full-time undergraduates, making it the largest program of its kind in the world. Testifying to its quality and success, it has been mimicked by more than 100 universities, colleges and secondary schools across Canada.

Waterloo boasts active links with some 2,600 businesses, industries and agencies across Canada and around the world. A classic win-win situation, the program in which students alternate classroom and lab time with course-related work terms allows young people to earn money and gain valuable experience while their employers gauge the on-the-job skills of prospective full-time employees.

Today, the University of Waterloo is one of Canada's most successful and prestigious universities, a destination of choice for the country's top students and an attractive place for professors to establish careers in teaching and research.

But 42 years ago, in its infancy, the University of Waterloo boasted only a pair of overcrowded buildings and a desire to produce a steady supply of well-trained engineers. As well, Waterloo also espoused an educational approach disdained by the country's academic establishment and a caution-to-the-wind attitude that would spawn a history of daring and innovation.

Launched in 1957 by a group of Kitchener-Waterloo businessmen, the school was held in "no esteem" in academic circles. Dr. Douglas Wright, 3rd president of the university and its first dean of engineering, says a then-handful of eager, young faculty members were anything but intimidated by such disregard. If anything, Wright recalls, the fledgling institution operated under an all-pervasive exuberance, a sense that anything could be attempted because there was nothing to lose.

A "license to be radical" is how Wright once put it. And so, despite predictions of failure and doom from traditional academic circles, the upstart university, eager for distinction, introduced Canada's first co-operative system of education.

On any given day, a UW co-op student might be found working two miles beneath the earth's surface in a South African diamond mine or in a Taiwan office building where trade representatives enhance Canada's overseas opportunities. He or she may be managing an arts facility or theatre, helping to plan urban and rural environments or extending the boundaries of an ever-widening computer frontier. The list, as they say, goes on. But there's much more to the University of Waterloo than its world-renowned co-op program. Situated on 1,000 acres of rolling, landscaped grounds covered with mature trees, lined with meandering streams and dotted with picturesque bridges, UW's complement of 14,500 full-time students can also choose to take the regular system of study (non co-op), and 109 program options in six faculties and four university colleges.

From its humble beginnings, UW has emerged as one of Canada's leading comprehensive universities, producing highly sought-after graduates in Arts and Science, Mathematics and Engineering, and Applied Health Sciences and Environmental Studies. Its alumni are now 100,000 strong and include everything from corporate CEOs and architects to optometrists and novelists. Indeed, UW's reputation as a research-intensive and academically innovative institution with high academic standards has made it a magnet for many of the best and brightest students from across Canada and around the world. (They are also among the most caring, raising over $100,000 annually in a variety of fundraising events for local charities and causes.)

Of particular note is the fact that a national reputational survey in *Maclean's* magazine has chosen UW #1 and best

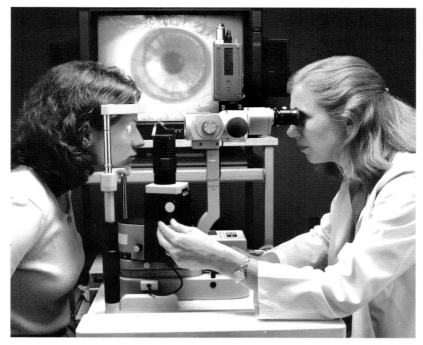

overall, most innovative and most likely to produce tomorrow's leaders for the past seven years.

With its 44 post-baccalaureate programs, 28 at the doctoral level, it has become one of the country's leading centres for graduate studies, attracting exemplary students who annually win more than their share of research awards. The school is increasingly regarded as a preferred destination among students seeking an international educational experience. Not only do UW researchers and students participate in a wide range of international graduate programs and research projects, but the school also boasts more than 50 inter-university exchange programs with institutions worldwide.

Waterloo is a research hotbed. As a consequence of the respect earned for its work in theoretical fields ranging from mathematics to the human psychology, and for the applied research and inventions that have been adapted for use in Canada and abroad, UW's researchers are awarded more than $50 million annually in research grants. Sources include major research councils such as the Social Science and Humanities Research Council, Natural Sciences and Engineering Research Council, plus special provincial and federal government grants and partnerships with business and industry. Here, over 800 faculty members continue to collaborate with post-doctorate fellows, students, technicians, staff and corporate and government partners, to produce a staggering collection of intellectual property.

As well, the school's many innovations go well beyond its groundbreaking co-op program. With the advent of the computer back in the early 1960s, UW became the first Canadian university to introduce the study of computing. That foresight has helped catapult UW among the world leaders in the burgeoning computer field. Not only are UW graduates seen as hot commodities by prospective employers in the computer industry, but the school has also become known as a world leader in the design and development of intellectual and educational software products used around the globe. In addition, the computer-related expertise developed here has generated scores of spin-off companies, many of them clustered around

the university, that focus on knowledge-based research and product development.

These companies, which have produced thousands of jobs, add hundreds of millions to the local economy and augment the significant impact of the university, already exceeding $340 million in direct and indirect spending.

Foresight also played a major role in the development of the country's first Faculty of Environmental Studies almost 30 years ago, a faculty that has become an acknowledged leader in environmental teaching and research in North America.

UW also pioneered innovations in distance education more than a quarter century ago with the creation of the first audio cassette university-level learning format. Today, complete degree programs are available in arts, environmental studies and science, and are accessible on the Internet. UW's distance education program now boasts more than 15,000 course registrations, essentially bringing the classroom to thousands of people who, for various reasons, can't come to the campus. At the same time, more than half a million non-students visit the campus each year to enjoy UW's many publicly accessible facilities, including an earth sciences museum that attracts thousands of school children annually.

Research, innovation, teaching excellence, high academic standards, community involvement. Small wonder Dr. James Downey, upon becoming UW's 4th president in 1993, made the remark that "Waterloo isn't just a university; it's an adventure."

And the adventure, as they like to say around this vibrant campus, continues. [◄►]

Waterloo's School of Optometry is a centre of leading-edge research in vision care.

The University of Waterloo introduced computer studies 40 years ago and remains one of North America's most outstanding centres of computer science research and education.

In fact, the large trophy case in the gleaming lobby of the company's Cambridge headquarters is filled with awards ATS has received over the years, awards from a number of major companies and government bodies recognizing its innovation, entrepreneurship, quality in design and excellence in performance.

All of which is testimony to the fact ATS stands ready to assist customers from conception to completion of a project, including the design phase, development, toolmaking and machining, programming, integration, assembly, installation, training and support. In fact, each phase of the process is accomplished in-house by its team of technical specialists and engineers who continually develop new automation products and integrate them with existing technology to provide solutions that routinely exceed customer expectations while delivering the highest return on investment.

This, quite simply, is a company that will go to virtually any lengths to meet a customer's needs. Only recently, for instance, ATS launched its advanced manufacturing division in response to the needs of a single customer producing a single product. To accommodate the customer, the company built a 160,000-square-foot facility, supplied its own management team, and designed automation systems capable of producing the component.

Not to be overlooked in ATS's willingness to go the extra mile, however, is its strong presence as a corporate citizen. It has been a major contributor to local hospitals, the arts, and educational institutions. In 1997, its employees gave more per capita to the

local United Way campaign than any other company in the area.

What does the future hold for ATS? The possibilities are limitless. The company is eyeing the possible expansion of automation systems in emerging markets such as health care, packaging and solar energy. It is also looking to its newly launched advanced manufacturing division as a catalyst to further business opportunities.

Above all, however, its future will continue to be linked with its past. From its very entry into the industrial automation industry, ATS has sought to meet manufacturers' requirements for systems with faster cycle times, more complex processes and fewer defects.

The company has provided the solutions time after time in the past. It will continue to do so in the future. ◪

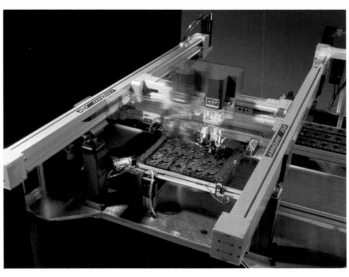

To many people, Bell Canada is simply regarded as the telephone company.

Which isn't surprising. Bell, after all, has been synonymous with the provision of telephone services in Canada for more than a century, and continues to increase the benefits and capabilities of Alexander Graham Bell's 1876 invention.

(above) Moving out old equipment for new technology.

(right) Bell Community Volunteers (formerly Bell Pioneers) repair Braillers for CNIB.

But Bell, whose local tradition also spans more than 100 years, is much more than a telephone company alone. The company, which employs some 700 people in the predominant CTT cities of Kitchener-Waterloo, Cambridge and Guelph, is also a renowned leader in the much broader field of telecommunications. And as the profound transformation of the telecommunications field continues, Bell, through strategic decisions, savvy investments, strong partnerships with the university community and innovative customer service, is prepared to retain that leadership role.

Not that Bell has lost sight of the telephone. The company is ever vigilant in its efforts to improve telephone service to its millions of subscribers across Ontario and Quebec. To wit: Bell's $180 million network modernization project that enhances service to one million customers in small and medium-sized communities throughout Ontario and Quebec. The project brings the benefits of fully modern digital switching to these rural and medium-sized communities, equipping them with telecommunication services similar to those in major urban centres—everything from call display to three-way-calling.

To Bell, however, the key to a prosperous future lies in its ability to provide customers with more than second-to-none telephone service. It envisions a future where high-speed services are the expectation in an environment where customers also seek greater simplicity and less fragmentation as they attempt to satisfy their varied and expanding communications requirements. It envisions a future where busy consumers will increasingly lament grappling with several companies and a number of bills in order to have those needs met.

Suffice it to say, Bell is working to provide the answers. Among its goals is to someday provide a simple, seamless, one-stop service that meets all the communications requirements of its customers, be it entertainment, internet, wireless or wireline. Indeed, Bell has already made significant strides towards that goal, thanks to a number of new services.

The company invested heavily, for instance, in ¨BCE Emergis™, one of North America's major players in the rapidly growing field of e-commerce. Through its ¨ExpressVU™ service, the company now boasts about 200,000 digital satellite television customers. ¨Sympatico™, with more than a half million customers, is the largest internet service in Canada. Meanwhile, Sympatico's high speed edition, which uses digital subscriber line technology, connects customers to the internet at speeds up to 30 times faster than conventional modems.

Much of the impetus for Bell's strategies and evolving services stems from what it calls a customer value approach to integration. In other words, listening to its customers and allowing them greater input in the ongoing search for ways to make their lives simpler.

Its customers have told Bell that they have become increasingly perplexed by the confusion of communications services and are tired of juggling and remembering office, home, cell phone, multiple voice mail box, home fax and e-mail numbers.

Bell listened. And the result is its "SimplyOne™ Service, which combines wireline and wireless—one's home phone, mobile and voice mail box all on the same number.

In another move to make things simpler for customers, Bell Canada combined with Bell Mobility to form a single integrated retail network. The company will establish 240 'Bell World/Espace Bell™ stores throughout Ontario and Quebec, providing a one-stop communications shopping environment where customers have ready access to the complete range of services.

Bell invests heavily in research and development, largely through strong partnerships with leading Canadian companies and, increasingly, with the university community. In fact, Bell, which considers universities as the "seedbed" for research, funds and supports a number of university research initiatives that will help keep it at the forefront of often mindboggling technological change.

It supports research at the University of Toronto which examines the effect of electromagnetic energy on sensitive electronics, for instance. At Carleton University, Bell helped fund the expansion of CHAT, the student/faculty electronic communication tool. It was involved in developing technology-enabled learning through the Queen's University faculty of education. And at Waterloo's Wilfrid Laurier University, Bell helped create a state-of-the-art videoconference facility.

But aside from its undisputed technological leadership and its diligent search for new and better ways to serve its customers, there's something else about Bell. Namely, that it has established itself as a strong corporate citizen, providing financial and volunteer support to an array of cultural, health, educational and civic activities throughout the country.

Through donations and volunteer efforts, the company has certainly supported a wide range of CTT organizations, including the United Way, the Kitchener-Waterloo Community Foundation, the Drayton Festival Theatre, Oktoberfest, Junior Achievement, St. John Ambulance, the Heart and Stroke Foundation, the Waterloo Region Track 3 Ski School for disabled skiers and many others too numerous to mention.

In addition, an altruistic army of more than 25,000 active and retired Bell employees dubbed "the Bell Pioneers" contributed more than 200,000 hours annually of volunteer effort to a number of community activities in Ontario and Quebec. Their main focus is on education programs, such as computers for schools. In fact, the pioneers have so far refurbished and distributed more than 15,000 computers to schools in the two provinces.

Bell's philanthropic endeavours should come as no surprise, however. The company has always believed in the inextricable link between its business interests and the well-being of the communities it serves.

And as Bell prepares to fortify its prominent telecommunications reputation into the next century, that belief is stronger than ever. [■]

* BCE Emergis is a trade-mark of BCE Inc. Bell Canada is a licensed user.
+ ExpressVU is a trade-mark of Bell ExpressVU Inc. Bell Canada is a licensed user.
** SimplyOne is a trade-mark of Sasktel used under licensed user.
≠ Sympatico is a trade-mark of Medialix Interactive. Bell Canada is a licensed user.
¥ Bell World and Espace Bell is a trade-mark of Bell Canada.

(above left) Launch of new Vista 450 (with e-mail) in Hamilton.

(below) High tech testing at our lab.

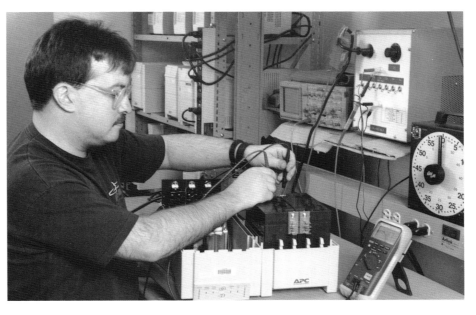

Students from this faculty have also left their mark in the annual Association for Computer Machinery Programming contest, a competition of similar stature in the computer science field. UW student teams won the world title in 1999 and 1994 as well as the east central regional finals in each of the last seven years. Waterloo has enjoyed top 10 finishes in other world finals including last year when it finished third in the world, while ranking first among North American schools.

All of which is testimony to a faculty that continues to attract the best and brightest young mathematical minds in the country, a faculty that offers its students a rich, robust and thorough education in all aspects of mathematics.

As a result, its graduates are vigorously recruited for top positions within major businesses and industries around the globe.

The faculty, which admits approximately 1,000 first-year stu-

Waterloo's bright young mathematicians annually rank at the top, with Harvard, Princeton and MIT in the prestigious Putnam competition.

The University of Waterloo's Faculty of Mathematics has earned more than its share of bragging rights since its inception more than 30 years ago.

It has grown, for instance, into the world's largest centre for education in the mathematical and computer sciences. It offers students a rich education that keeps them on the cutting edge of developments in the mathematical field. It continues to nurture strong partnerships with industry through its high quality co-operative education program, the outstanding achievements of its gifted students and the research accomplishments of its professors.

Students from this faculty continue to shine each year as they match their skills against counterparts from over 400 of North America's universities in the highly acclaimed Putnam mathematics competitions. Both its three-member teams, as well as a host of individual students who participate, have consistently ranked in the top 5 and top 10 alongside highly reputed schools such as Harvard, Princeton and MIT.

In fact, a UW team of students has finished among the top five six times within the last decade. And only Harvard and MIT have consistently placed as many or more individual competitors among the top 200 and the top 500.

dents annually and now boasts over 3,000 undergraduates, was founded in 1967. And since UW was the first university to collect all the mathematical sciences, place them under a single umbrella and give them faculty status, it was a highly unique move at the time. It was also far more visionary than people realized then. The move was important because it gave the mathematical sciences unprecedented prominence, size and stature.

The faculty offers a wide range of programs. Not only does it boast world-renowned programs in actuarial and computer science, but the faculty is also highly recognized for its offerings in pure and applied mathematics, accounting, business administration, operations research and statistics. At the same time, its department of combinatorics and optimization is world-famous for its unique concentration of expertise in applied mathematical areas that are intimately related to computer science. For the uninitiated, the application of combinatorics and optimization is as diverse as planning the efficient layout of a factory floor to improving telecommunication signals.

And because these programs are interlinked and administered within a single faculty, students here enjoy ready access to a wide medley of mathematics courses. As a result, they graduate as extensively prepared, well-rounded and highly versatile employees. Computer science graduates leave Waterloo with solid math skills, for example. Conversely, mathematics students will graduate having had extensive exposure to computer science.

The decision to create one large faculty has also heightened the intellectual environment for faculty members. Because today, within two linked buildings, more than 140 mathematicians of all stripes readily collaborate on any number of projects, creating a highly fertile and diverse research atmosphere. Each year, faculty members receive millions in grants from industry and government to conduct research in everything from the fundamentals of number theory to the development of methods that enhance analysis of large databases.

Many companies that have sprung up around the university have emanated from research projects launched within this faculty. These companies, most of whom lie within the burgeoning information technology field, now employ thousands of people and contribute hundreds of millions of dollars to the local economy. Outstanding success stories of publicly traded companies actively participating in the education of UW students include Certicom, Open Text, Mortice Kern Systems, Research In Motion and Waterloo Maple.

Another unique aspect of UW's math program is its extensive and high-quality co-op program, something Dr. Alan

George, the faculty's dean, calls a "mutual test drive," for both students and potential employers. Indeed, George says UW students are eagerly recruited for challenging co-op jobs throughout Canada and abroad, including actuarial duties in major insurance companies, development of software within the financial services and governments or data analysis for major banks and corporations.

Finally, UW's math faculty has become a leader in the promotion of mathematics at the elementary and high school levels. More than 200,000 Canadian students from Grade 7 to final year in high school, now participate in faculty-sponsored mathematics contests each year. In fact, many senior high school students participate in these contests in order to be considered for one of UW's substantial entrance scholarships, or to meet admission standards.

The contests really have two purposes. First, they are designed to attract students to the challenge of solving mathematical puzzles and problems. Secondly, the contests allow the faculty to form ongoing relationships with mathematics teachers, and to identify the best young mathematical minds across the country.

Small wonder Canadian high school graduates with serious mathematics-related aspirations have come to view UW's math faculty as the ultimate venue for their ongoing studies. [➡]

World Champions—UW's winners of the 1999 ACM International collegiate programming contest: Prof. Gordon Comack (coach), Viet-Trung Luu, David Kennedy and Andrej Lhotak.

While it's impossible to measure in exact terms, it's safe to say that the University of Waterloo's Faculty of Applied Health Sciences has had a rather significant impact on preventive health care in North America.

For one thing, its graduates continue to make their mark in hospitals, nursing homes, clinics and workplaces across the continent. For another, its professors are internationally recognized for their expertise and the groundbreaking research that has helped refine the techniques of practitioners throughout the field.

gain invaluable career-related experience in real workplace settings through a wide variety of high quality co-operative education opportunities.

What's more, kinesiology is the only department of its type to offer an option in ergonomics, a huge and emerging field necessitated by industry's growing concern with the escalating costs of employee absenteeism and injury. As a result, companies throughout North America are knocking on the department's door, eager to land its graduates, many of whom are already modifying jobs and machinery to enhance safety and efficiency in workplaces across the continent.

In fact, the department is playing a leading research role in the field. Among other things, it is involved in a five-year, $2-million study investigating work-related factors that increase the risk of low-back pain in the automobile industry.

Small wonder that students who graduate from this faculty can invariably look forward to a wide range of career opportunities. Indeed, they employ their formidable knowledge and skills in hospitals and nursing homes, in rehabilitation programs or clinics that assess movement and musculoskeletal function. They enhance health and safety in industry, prescribe exercise and fitness regimens for both the weekend athlete and the elite performer, modify living environments for the elderly, enhance quality of life for the disabled . . . the list goes on.

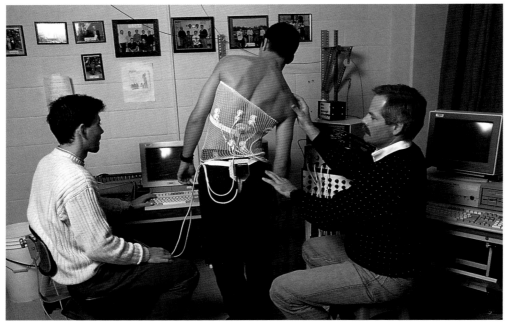

Applied Health Sciences researchers focus on injury prevention and health promotion.

The faculty, with its 1,000 undergraduates, 150 graduate students and 50 professors, focuses all its research, teaching and community outreach initiatives on a singular goal—to enhance human health and well-being by seeking to prevent disease and injury, preserve and promote health, optimize physical abilities, help individuals cope with disability and improve quality of life.

Among other things, the faculty boasts Canada's first and largest department of kinesiology, an area that investigates the mechanisms and principles of human movement. The department's dynamic professors offer the largest variety of kinesiology courses in Canada, while producing an impressive volume of crucial research in areas ranging from catastrophic injury prevention to balance and gait control in the elderly. Each year, in fact, the department's professors receive some $1 million in grants and contracts to conduct basic and applied research. Invariably, their findings are published in leading national and international journals. Several researchers have written books or book chapters related to their areas of expertise.

The AHS faculty prides itself on the cutting-edge education offered to students, a significant percentage of whom

The faculty's Lyle S. Hallman Institute for Health Promotion also has a profound impact on the local community and all Canadians through its outstanding graduates and a variety of research activities and public outreach initiatives. They include: the Kenneth G. Murray Alzheimer Research and Education Program; research into children's sedentary lifestyles and risk of early heart disease; adults recovering from heart attacks through the Hardy Harts program; cancer research and programs to help the effectiveness of smoking cessation programs; research in helping seniors avoid falls and public programs examining general population fitness and nutrition.

Not that the faculty intends to rest on its laurels. Its never-ending search for new and innovative ways to fulfill its mandate, and its ability to produce a steady stream of industry-leading graduates guarantees that the faculty will continue to place its unique stamp on the preventive health care field. ■

UNIVERSITY OF WATERLOO ENVIRONMENTAL STUDIES

When it comes to its size, the University of Waterloo's Faculty of Environmental Studies can't compare to much larger faculties like engineering and mathematics.

But when it comes to reputation and global impact, this 30-year-old faculty, among the first of its kind in Canada, need not take a back seat to anyone.

Residents in and around Ontario's Algonquin National Park would vouch for that. Thanks to ground-breaking research conducted under the auspices of UW's environmental studies faculty, these residents now realize that a smooth coexistence with the area's wolf population is a distinct possibility.

And, thanks to UW's environmental studies researchers, the Chinese government possesses a much greater ability to effectively manage its coastline in terms of tourism and ecology.

Seeking sustainability in a world where much of what humans do is unsustainable, the Faculty of Environmental Studies was founded in 1969. Other environmental studies programs have sprung up across Canada since then. But it's a safe bet that there will be a UW graduate on their teaching rosters.

Today, the faculty boasts 1,200 undergraduate students. It includes two professional schools—architecture and planning—and two academic departments—geography as well as environment and resource studies. Each school or department has left its own indelible mark in its respective disciplines.

For instance, an accreditation team of Canadian, American and Mexican architects recently ranked UW's school of architecture among the top 10 programs of its kind in North America. Certainly, its students routinely bring home top awards in some of the world's most prestigious architecture and design competitions: competitions open to practising professionals as well as students. In the last six years, for instance, UW architecture students have won four governor-general awards in architecture. Students from this professional school of architecture have captured many honours in similar competitions in various other countries, including Finland and Ireland.

UW's school of planning, meanwhile, has heavily influenced municipal and regional planning departments across Canada. In fact, more UW planning graduates occupy key positions in the country's planning departments than those of any other institution.

The other departments are also world-renowned, whether for their pioneering work in areas such as geographic information systems and remote sensing, or for basic research into everything from climate change to sea ice distribution.

Environmental Studies is also respected for its research. Each year its 60 faculty members and 200 graduate students share some $2 million in research grants from both government and the private sector.

Dr. Geoff McBoyle, the faculty's dean, vows that research intensity will continue to grow. McBoyle says the variety and

depth of research is inextricably linked with the quality of education the faculty can offer its students.

Due to this excellence in research, the environmental studies faculty continues to attract top graduate students from across Canada. These students, McBoyle explains, bring the creativity and cutting-edge ideas that are quickly integrated into the classroom.

But as far as faculty officials are concerned, the best testimony to its high quality comes from the students who have studied here.

McBoyle cites a recent survey of environmental studies alumni in which 98 per cent of the respondents, most of them embedded in challenging careers within government and the private sector, enthusiastically endorsed the education they received here. What's more, they would highly recommend the program to prospective students who are searching for careers in which they can make a difference to society. ◼

Waterloo is a world leader in wetlands and ground-water research.

Originating in June 1997, Communitech, officially known as CTT's Community Technology Association, is the result of countless discussions between representatives of more than a dozen organizations. Communitech is the partnership of technology and technology service companies, educational institutions and all levels of government working together to encourage the development and sharing of technology resources within Canada's Technology Triangle (CTT). Communitech is recognized as a dynamic and unified voice on behalf of the area's technology industry.

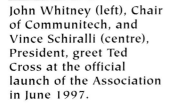

John Whitney (left), Chair of Communitech, and Vince Schiralli (centre), President, greet Ted Cross at the official launch of the Association in June 1997.

The Association focuses on four key areas of delivery, referred to as TEAM—Technology, Education, Advocacy and Marketing. The overall objective of the Association is: to enhance access to state-of-the-art technology essential for area companies to compete on a global basis; to help build a stronger membership through various training and educational initiatives; to articulate the needs of the technology sector to target groups including all levels of government and to market and promote the CTT as a desirable location to invest, work, live and play.

Certainly, Communitech's success in each of these areas has raised more than a few eyebrows. The membership, that includes the who's who of the CTT, exceeded the targeted goal of 100 members by the end of the organization's first fiscal year, a total rivaling long-established associations in much larger areas.

Communitech offers services that include: highly popular luncheons where members have the opportunity to hear and learn from industry leaders, career fairs encouraging school-age children to pursue education in the field of technology and peer-to-peer support programs. In addition to these services, Communitech acts as a quiet lobbying entity on behalf of its membership to ensure the needs of the technology sector are heard.

Not only have these services and programs drawn rave reviews and enthusiastic feedback from the association's membership, they have attracted noteworthy attention from outside the area as well. Communitech gained notoriety in a well-known Canadian magazine, Canadian Business, just months after the association's official launch.

"We haven't been around very long, but already the word's out that this community supports its technology industry," says Vince Schiralli, Communitech's spirited president.

Although CTT already enjoys the reputation as a desirable area in which to do business, the activities and accomplishments of Communitech broaden the CTT profile and lend to the attraction of new technology businesses to the triangle.

"If you're in the technology business, says Schiralli, where do you want to be? Most likely you want to be where there is structure and support, where there are weekly and monthly meetings and events related to your business and where there is a collective voice to represent your concerns. I can tell you the CTT and Communitech is where it's happening." ▮◆

Communitech staff, from left to right, Chris O'Brien, Vince Schiralli, Cindy Pearson, Lori Ridgway.

DALSA CORPORATION

CCD image capture technology has become a $2-billion business worldwide, a burgeoning field where ongoing innovation has created the potential for a seemingly limitless number of high-speed applications.

And a rapidly growing Waterloo company called DALSA Inc. has become widely recognized as one of the foremost leaders in the design and manufacture of high-performance CCD cameras and silicon chips.

For the uninitiated, CCD stands for charge coupled device. In layman's terms, it's a photosensitive silicon chip that converts photons to electrons and moves them serially through proprietary video electronics to capture images and readable information.

Dr. Savvas Chamberlain was among the pioneering researchers in the field when he founded DALSA Inc. in 1980. Chamberlain, a University of Waterloo professor, formed DALSA as a contract research and development company with an eye towards the eventual commercialization of the technology he helped cultivate.

By 1990 DALSA had introduced its own camera family and had become a product-oriented company. Today, 95 per cent of DALSA's products are sold to original equipment manufacturers in Asia, Europe, the United States and Canada. Many of its customers are multinational corporations firmly embedded on the Fortune 500 list.

Meanwhile, DALSA's revenues surpassed $27 million last year. And for the past five years, the now-public company has enjoyed annual revenue and profit growth of 35 per cent.

Company officials credit DALSA's outstanding reputation for innovation. DALSA, they'll tell you, has never been content to rest on its laurels, formidable as they may be. Company officials know that long-term success depends on DALSA's ongoing ability to enhance existing technologies, develop others and find ways to continually increase the cost performance of their products.

It's that very attitude that continues to attract top quality scientists and engineers to the company. So dedicated is DALSA to innovation, that one quarter of its 200 employees and 20 per cent of its annual revenues are dedicated solely to research and development.

Consequently, DALSA's products are often the first to reach the market and continue to set the benchmark in the burgeoning high-performance imaging business.

Thanks to DALSA's innovation, CCD technology is being used in a number of invaluable applications these days.

Among other things, they are being used for postal sorting, document management, electronics inspection and machine vision applications.

In all, DALSA offers over 100 modular expandable cameras using CCD image sensors which provide the ultimate in spatial resolution and responsivity with the highest data transfer speed found anywhere in the industry.

One of DALSA's particular strengths is that both the image sensor and the camera electronics are manufactured in-house. That has given the company the technological know-how and scientific depth to help meet the individual imaging challenges of its customers.

What does the future hold for DALSA? Company officials are braced for ongoing growth as adoption of CCD imaging continues to expand into new applications.

DALSA will continue to push the performance limits of imaging technology as they seek solutions for their customers. [■]

Founded in 1994 by David Popowich, Second Foundation specializes in the sale, implementation and customization of Platinum Financial Accounting Software.

As a Chartered Accountant with 12 years public accounting experience at Price-Warehouse, David supervised many successful Platinum installations. David was a partner in a Toronto-based consulting firm before applying his expertise to his own company. By hiring top quality staff, David has built the framework for Second Foundation to enjoy continuous growth providing enterprise-wide business solutions to the high-profile mid-market. Second Foundation has earned a reputation as a customer-centric leader in the financial accounting industry.

Second Foundation's reputation is built on the philosophy that a successful software implementation involves the assessment of their client's unique business requirements and the tailoring of the software to meet those requirements. Second Foundation's methodology begins with a thorough analysis of their client's business and in-house procedures. After analyzing the options available, a solution is architected. Second Foundation then assembles a project team to make the solution a reality. Each project draws on the resources and expertise of client personnel, consultants, programmers and technologists to ensure a properly tailored and smooth integration. Using the latest industry tools, their project team customizes the solution, and in some cases, creates add-ons to handle specialized or strategic aspects of a client's business or industry. Once the system successfully goes live, team members remain available to clients to provide both telephone and on-site support.

David Popowich, President and CEO.

After project end, Second Foundation provides further expertise to address new client business and technology requirements that may arise. Clients enjoy a positive, beneficial relationship with Second Foundation. One high-profile national company attests to their "accessibility, positive responsiveness and courteous professionalism...that go beyond the expectations of a normal support group." Another client notes that "it's a rare occasion when the CEO of a company can be reached off-hours...Second Foundation has continually provided us with fast and accurate turn-around to all of our questions."

Second Foundation's commitment to excellence also extends to its involvement with the Kitchener-Waterloo community as evidenced through the use of local services and businesses for all in-house needs, support of staff involvement with charitable and service organizations, and its strong ties with the local universities and colleges.

David Popowich, a graduate of Wilfrid Laurier University, holds the belief that there is a strong link between success in business and education. Second Foundation actively hires co-op students from Wilfrid Laurier University and the University of Waterloo each term, and has also accepted placement students from other college and government programs. Students, encouraged to learn and develop their skills in peer relationships with other employees, excel and rise to the challenges, complexities and responsibilities of their jobs. As an extra benefit, their valuable business experience lends context and meaning to their academic studies. Second Foundation's university involvement includes providing Platinum Software at no cost to the School of Accountancy at the University of Waterloo and allowing the company to be the basis for a term project for a fourth-year Rhetoric and Professional Writing class.

Second Foundation's strong customer-service philosophy depends on a team of highly skilled employees, providing quality business advice, a belief in strong ideals and a carefully planned growth strategy. Second Foundation continues to develop new ways to meet the evolving needs of the business community through the creative use of new technologies and business techniques. [■]

AGRI-FOOD LABORATORIES

There are two basic ways farmers and agriculture dealers can determine how soil or feed will perform under certain conditions.

They can hazard an educated guess, of course, and take their chances. Or, thanks to advancing technologies that help provide fast, accurate information about such things as nutrient levels, they can be absolutely certain.

Clearly, the rapid growth of Guelph's Agri-Food Laboratories, whose motto is "Providing Measurements for Management," indicates that the latter is fast becoming the wise and preferred option.

Agri-Food Laboratories, which relies heavily on cutting edge technology, provides the definitive documentation farmers and agriculture dealers find indispensable amid today's economic realities.

The lab is the descendent of Griffiths Laboratories, launched in 1984 as a first-of-a-kind, contract lab for the Ontario Ministry of Agriculture and Food. Six years later, as the lab began to shift to a user-pay format, it was purchased by the current owners, Dale Cowan and his wife, Karon Tracey-Cowan.

Since then the full-service lab, which provides highly detailed soil, feed and greenhouse testing, as well as feed and fertilizer quality control programs, fertilizer analysis, toxins screening, compost testing and livestock water suitability, has grown from nine to 31 employees. The largest privately owned, independent testing facility in the province, Agri-Food's Imperial Road headquarters has grown from 4,000 to 10,000 square feet. It has also enjoyed a six-fold increase in sales, boasts the lion's share of the Ontario market and lists among its customers some of the largest agriculture dealers in the country.

Among other things, customers have responded to the lab's absolute commitment to quality. Accredited by both Agriculture Canada and the Ontario Ministry of Agriculture and Food, the lab uses the latest analytical equipment to help it meet the most stringent internal and external quality control standards.

The lab also adheres to a customer-driven philosophy, which means it stands ready to conform to the individual needs and requirements of its customers, not the other way around.

When customers seek the services of Agri-Food Laboratories, they also know they are dealing with a company known for its innovation as well as its highly efficient use of groundbreaking technology.

Agri-Food is the first lab, for example, to offer services in comprehensive soil sampling and the first to offer extensive Geographic Information Systems (GIS) mapping capabilities in Ontario and Quebec. At the same time, its Global Positioning Satellite (GPS) expertise has allowed it to coordinate a wide range of variable rate applications and extensive test plots for corn, soybeans, tobacco and alfalfa.

The search for new technological advantages, however, continues. The highly trained, top-level chemists, technicians and customer service personnel who staff this lab know that the efficient use of cutting edge technology can only enhance their ability to serve their customers.

Certainly, they know that the ongoing pursuit of innovation is the key to further customization of reporting and analysis procedures. And that can only enhance Agri-Food's already pronounced ability to meet the individual specifications of its customers, maximizing their economic potential amid the rapidly changing demands of agriculture.

In short, the lab's passion for quality, its absolute commitment to the customer and its ongoing quest for new and better ways of doing business is Agri-Food's recipe for a highly successful future of continued growth and exemplary service to the agricultural community. ▣

(top)Agri-Food Laboratories.

(bottom) Soybean Field.
Photo by Mike Grandmaison.

Photo by Mike Grandmaison.

CHAPTER NINE

Manufacturing, Distribution & Construction

9

Photo by Mike Grandmaison

GLENOIT CORPORATION

Midway through the 19th century, a rather eccentric professor and rugged outdoorsman—surname Glen—was achieving legendary status through his bold explorations into North America's still unknown wilderness.

As legends invariably will, Professor Glen enthralled his admirers with the occasional pearl of wisdom for posterity. Such as his motto—"Stand judged by the fibre of your character . . . and the character of your fibre."

The venerable adventurer didn't know it at the time, of course, but some 140 years later his credo continues to shape the success of a major North American fabric company which is creating a rather formidable reputation of its own. The company is Glenoit Corporation, the largest manufacturer of pile (sliver knit) fabrics in North America. Its officials were so enamoured with Professor Glen's qualities they dubbed its latest line of fabric GlenPile.

The company was founded in Beloit, Wisconsin, in 1955 and moved to Tarboro, N.C., in 1960. Today, the privately-owned company boasts three mills and more than 1,800 employees throughout North America. Most recently—in August, 1997—the company moved into Canada when it acquired the former Borg division of Collins & Aikman, which had developed a strong tradition itself during 50 years of pile fabric production in Elmira, a picturesque, traditional town of tree-lined streets and stately homes.

The original Berber by Glenoit—the distinctively soft and friendly pile.

To the 150 Elmira employees who owe their livelihood to this modern 130,000-square-foot production facility, Glenoit's move is regarded as welcome news indeed. After all, Glenoit is known for its homespun pride, its emphasis on quality and a business savvy that has helped it strengthen each and every operation it has acquired. Since acquiring the Elmira plant last year, for instance, Glenoit has invested heavily in new, state-of-the-art machinery that has significantly enhanced its already strong production capabilities.

In acquiring the Elmira plant, headquarters for the Glenoit Corporation of Canada, Glenoit not only establishes a firm presence in Canada but also lands a full production facility where the rough fiber is dyed, blended, carded, knitted, finished and packaged. The plant currently produces about 13,000 metres of fabric per day, most of which is earmarked

Technically advanced GlenPile®—a perfect mix of performance and relaxed style.

for the outdoor, sportswear and apparel markets. But the fabric produced here is also used in a variety of other products, including rugs, golf bag linings, bed throws, automotive interiors, toys, powder puffs, saddle bags, home furnishings—even paint rollers.

Like Glenoit's other mills, the Elmira plant operates under the same expectation of quality and innovation, a combination that helped the company achieve record sales last year.

Although Glenoit has always enjoyed a strong reputation for quality, its position as North America's major producer of pile fabrics has largely been established this decade, however, with the overwhelmingly successful launch of a trio of sliver knit products.

In 1993, the company launched its Berber line, gradually expanding its pattern options. Today, this fabric, whose hair fibres give it a warm and rugged appearance, making it ideal for an active lifestyle, is the single biggest fabric the company makes and appeals to major customers such as Polo, Jones New York, Woolrich, Liz Claiborne, Nautica, Columbia and many more.

A year after Berber's introduction, the company launched Glenaura, a dressier and more sophisticated fabric whose smooth and clean-cut appearance helped the company make immediate headway in the sports and outerwear markets.

In 1996, Glenoit launched GlenPile, a highly insulative pile that replaced pure polyester with a blend of polyester and microfibres to become what the company refers to as "the fabric made from fibre." Unlike insulated fabrics whose fibres are twisted into yarns before knitting, GlenPile's carefully selected fibres are permanently secured in the construction of fine guage knit, thereby allowing each fibre to work independently and much more efficiently.

In any case, the introduction of these three pile lines is the result of a company decision to place its future growth in the hands of microfibres. Until then, the company was largely known as a major fakefur, slipper, toy, rug and mat producer. Microfibres, however, were seen as a way of making major inroads in the burgeoning outdoor and sportswear apparel markets.

Seven years ago, the company began to refine its techniques to accommodate a future in microfibres. It purchased new equipment and modified old ones. It endured a period of considerable transition. But in hindsight, the move is seen as a major turning point. In fact, Glenoit's products now comprise 80 per cent of North America's sliver knit business.

Another secret to Glenoit's success, however, lies in the knitting process. Its investment in state-of-the-art jacquard knitting machines enables unlimited repeats on the fabric for added manufacturing ease, miminized loss and the ability to mix the various fibres and colours in an infinite number of ways.

Acquisitions and product expansion have also played a significant role in Glenoit's growth. In 1995, the corporation purchased the Borg Textile plant facility in Tennessee, a major competitor that had financial problems. Today, with updated equipment, the plant is flourishing and produces much of Glenoit's product lines.

In addition to its more recent acquisition in Elmira, Glenoit recently completed a $10-million expansion of its Tarboro facility, creating 60 new jobs for local residents in the process. In all, Glenoit now owns over a million square feet of North American production space.

But don't think Glenoit's outstanding success has left any

room for complacency. Housed in its Tarboro mill are its second-to-none design and testing laboratories, containing the most sophisticated computer equipment, which is operated by dedicated, top quality researchers. Indeed, the development of new colours, patterns, textures, weights and fibre blends for its luxurious, functional pile fabrics is a never-ending process at Glenoit. Among other things, Glenoit researchers have recently been working to develop a new, washable and itch-free wool fabric, called Microlana, which was expected to be introduced in the fall of 1998.

What does the future hold for this rapidly growing company? Further growth, Glenoit officials believe. And an ever-increasing presence in the outdoor sports apparel market.

Certainly, Glenoit's growth, success and innovation spell new challenges and new opportunities for the Elmira employees who lend their dedication and expertise to a now-flourishing plant that had struggled noticeably under its previous ownership. [◾▶]

Sophisticated Glenaura®—luxuriously light, warm and soft to the touch.

Glenoit Faux Furs—extra-ordinarily soft and sleek, they look and feel like the real thing.

Thanks to highly skilled, dedicated employees, the company has earned an international reputation for high quality products and services.

Cambridge-based Babcock & Wilcox Canada, one of Waterloo Region's largest employers, is world-renown in the design and manufacture of steam generation products and services.

Babcock & Wilcox Canada is a leader in the Canadian fossil boiler service and construction industry, the dominant supplier of replacement steam generators to the U.S. nuclear power market and a forerunner in the international nuclear equipment supply and services field.

The company is a very successful division of the Babcock & Wilcox Company in Barberton, Ohio. This, in turn, is a wholly-owned subsidiary of New Orleans-based McDermott International, Inc., a multinational corporation specializing in energy-related industries including offshore oil technology, marine construction and power generation.

Babcock & Wilcox Canada's roots in Waterloo Region date back to the 1844 inception of the Dumfries Foundry on the banks of the Grand River in the former town of Galt. In 1859, a pair of businessmen, John Goldie and Hugh McCulloch purchased this foundry. Under the name of Goldie & McCulloch, the enterprise manufactured vaults for general commerce, machinery for sugar and barrel making, plus steam engines and boilers for mill and factory use. After incorporating in 1981, the company began to concentrate on steam engines,

boilers, heaters and special plate work for both Canadian and worldwide markets.

While Goldie & McCulloch prospered in Canada, The Babcock & Wilcox Company of New York was establishing itself as a leader in the boiler business. Not only did George Babcock and Steven Wilcox obtain a patent for the water tube steam boiler in 1867, but one of their boilers also powered the dynamo for Thomas Edison's early incandescent lighting experiments.

In 1923, Goldie & McCulloch Co. Ltd. amalgamated with Babcock & Wilcox, a merger that would prove highly fruitful for the next several decades. Under the new name of Babcock-Wilcox & Goldie-McCulloch Limited, the company enjoyed steady growth while building a strong reputation for quality and innovation in the boiler industry.

Then, in 1967, shortly after Goldie-McCulloch sold its interests, the company was renamed Babcock & Wilcox Ltd. The current owners, McDermott International Inc., bought the company in 1978.

With more than 155 years of operating in Cambridge, Babcock & Wilcox Canada has helped cement the foundation of the community. The building blocks of a proud tradition—a glowing track record of quality, innovation and an ongoing desire to exceed industry standards—continue to be laid today in the company's current headquarters at the corner of Hespeler Road and Coronation Boulevard.

Today, Babcock & Wilcox Canada employs more than 1,500 at two manufacturing locations (one here in Cambridge, the other in Melville, Saskatchewan), five sales and services offices and several construction sites across Canada. Their local facilities span more than 570,000 square feet and boast the world's largest clean room for the assembly of nuclear steam generators. The 37,000-square-foot room is pressurized with filtered air to maintain a clean work environment minimizing the risk of contaminating steam generator internals.

In 1894, this Coronation Boulevard landmark was a small off-site manufacturing shop. Today, Babcock & Wilcox Canada's facility spans more than 490,000 square feet.

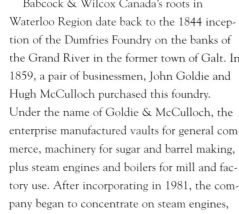

A recent addition to the facility is a modern welding and industrial skills training centre where in-house welding specialists learn the latest technologies and procedures. In 1999, the Ontario Ministry of Education and Training certified the centre as a vocational welder training facility. The centre also houses mechanical testing and metallographic laboratories for state-of-the-art welding development. As a result, the company, which predominantly works with specially selected metals, has pioneered a long list of welding techniques that have continually advanced industry standards.

Babcock & Wilcox Canada services the worldwide nuclear utility marketplace, as well as the Canadian steam generation market in the utility, pulp and paper, petrochemical and industrial sectors. Customers include power plants, pulp mills, refineries, processing plants, hospitals, universities and some of the world's major manufacturers.

The Canadian company has served the nuclear steam generator market with distinction for some 40 years. Not only do its steam generators drive the electrical turbines in every nuclear power plant in Canada, but with more than 230 nuclear steam generators spanning the globe, it has become the world leader in supplying replacement nuclear steam generators.

To its customers, the Babcock & Wilcox name has become synonymous with outstanding quality, and its exemplary reputation emanates largely from the dedication, skills and passion of its highly skilled, carefully selected and thoroughly trained employees.

In fact, in 1998, McDermott hired a major U.S. consulting firm to conduct a detailed economic analysis of Babcock & Wilcox's four North American manufacturing facilities. The consultants gave the Cambridge plant very high ratings for its productivity, safety record, product quality, superior work culture and union-management relationship. As a result, the Babcock & Wilcox Company reallocated some manufacturing work from the United States to its Canadian facilities creating additional jobs for skilled labour.

The consulting firm could also have applauded the company's heavy emphasis on training and innovation. Recognizing that its highly skilled workforce requires continuous training and learning to be competitive, Babcock & Wilcox Canada invests heavily in that regard. Indeed, the company is among the top one-third of Canadian companies who benchmark their training as a percentage of payroll.

Consequently, Babcock & Wilcox Canada is the only two-time winner of the City of Cambridge's Mayor's Award for excellence in workplace training. Since winning the award in 1994, the company added

leading-edge training practices to its already established base of programs to recapture the award in 1998. To crown off these successes, Babcock & Wilcox Canada was named Waterloo Region's Business of the Year in the fall of 1998. This award recognizes the company's demonstration of excellence in all areas including: exceptional corporate citizenship, a history of innovative products/services, leading-edge marketing strategies, outstanding customer service, high quality standards and excellent employee relations.

Indeed the Babcock & Wilcox Canada story is anything but over. By continuously improving all aspects of its business to reflect a rapidly evolving marketplace, this company has passed the test of time. Driven by the ideas and commitment of its employees, Babcock & Wilcox Canada seems destined to thrive and maintain a long prosperous future. [■]

(top) Steam generators and boilers fill the boiler shop of the country's largest manufacturer of steam generation products.

(center) Nuclear steam generators stand six stories tall, weigh between 250 and 800 tons, and have components manufactured to tolerances of 5/10,000th of an inch.

A once-well-known household moving company that was in need of transportation experience was purchased in 1987 by Walter and Joanne Scott. The company, McArthur Moving, was operating out of tiny, austere quarters on Cambridge's Hespeler Road, its assets reduced to a single tractor-trailer in dire need of repair if not outright replacement.

McArthur Express' 35,000 square feet, 10 acre facility located on Werlich Drive, Cambridge, Ontario.

To say that the company has been rejuvenated since the arrival of the Scotts would be an understatement. The company is still in Cambridge, but everything else has changed, and changed for the better. Now called McArthur Express, its headquarters are ensconced in a modern, 35,000-square-foot facility that sits on more than 10 acres of land on Werlich Drive. And it's no longer involved in the household moving business.

Today McArthur Express wields a stellar reputation as a specialist that distributes home and office furniture, store fixtures and high-value products. This vibrant enterprise, which has amassed a growing list of long-term customers, has 85 employees, 80 trucks and 180 trailers. All the vehicles are emblazoned with the logo of a Pony Express rider which is fitting since service and efficiency have become the hallmark of this organization.

Walter Scott, the president of McArthur Express, has been up to his elbows in all facets of the transportation business for over 35 years, and during that time he has learned a few things about customer service. He has held a number of management and supervisory positions, set up successful trucking operations for companies in Canada and the United States and prior to purchasing his latest enterprise, owned and operated a successful company that hauled office furniture all over North America.

All that experience has taught him one thing—customers and employees are the key to a successful business and this certainly applies to McArthur Express. Adhering to old-fashioned values and embracing the spirit of the Pony Express, McArthur Express is a family-owned-and- operated enterprise that is staffed by a collection of highly dedicated employees who are all treated like members of a close-knit family.

McArthur Express has forged an enviable record for its ability to expedite office furniture and high-tech equipment throughout Ontario, and the United States. And it does this safely, efficiently, and on time. It has achieved a pattern of continued, steady growth by concentrating on its specialty and doing it better than anyone else.

The company's services include truckload and less-than-truckload deliveries and pick-ups. With a dispatch service that operates 24 hours a day and seven days a week, it can handle any emergency and/or expedited shipment that comes its way and, what's more, distribute multiple shipments throughout the United States.

McArthur Express will blanket wrap, take on direct deliveries to installation sites and run expedited deliveries for trade shows and exhibits. Of course, its ever-growing fleet of trailers are air-ride and come fully equipped with all the necessities for damage-free delivery. Shipments are also closely monitored each step of the way, thereby providing customers with up-to-the-minute status reports. "Customer service is something that just can't be compromised. It's vital to everything we do," says Walter Scott.

According to Scott, one of the strengths that sets McArthur Express apart from its competitors is this: the ability of its highly trained employees to analyze the product being shipped and then determine the equipment and mode of handling necessary to ensure damage-free delivery.

Indeed, the company's high level of performance is testimony to the fact that its employees have enthusiastically embraced Walter and Joanne Scott's "go-the-extra-mile" attitude to customer service. In a recent survey of its customers, McArthur Express drew rave reviews for its consistently superior performance. Customers who were surveyed also gave the company's neatly uniformed, courteous and helpful drivers the highest marks.

"We have a number of employees who have reached ten years of service with us and we like to recognize such dedication," Walter Scott says. "Our success is truly due to the efforts and loyalty of many people."

To the Scotts, the pursuit of excellence and a preoccupation with outstanding customer service aren't

ees are continually trained and updated on the latest developments in safety and vehicle inspections. McArthur Express even requires an extensive post-trip inspection of all vehicles before they can return to the spacious loading docks through the fully secured gates. After each trip, vehicles must pass through the company's 'safety lane' where both truck and trailer undergo an exhaustive inspection. And before hitting the road again, the vehicles undergo yet another inspection of equal vigour.

The Scotts also have another motive for investing heavily in a company

(left) McArthur's family of employees assembled on the front lawn of their head office.

(bottom) Office furniture shipped from the manufacturer, staged at the terminal for furtherance into the United States.

only about growth and profitability. The efforts to build a reputable, first-class operation also stem from a desire to regain some of the respect lost in an industry that has been taken to task in the past; it seemed that too many owners and operators placed profits ahead of key concerns like driver professionalism, truck maintenance and road safety. Again, these are things that the Scotts refuse to compromise.

In fact, such commodities are among the linchpins of McArthur Express. Its state-of-the-art headquarters contains extensive maintenance and truck-wash facilities. The employ-

that is now assured of continued growth and prosperity. McArthur Express will remain a dynamic family enterprise since their two daughters, both of whom have been heavily involved in the enterprise for many years, will continue to build upon the solid traditions of excellence created by its founders. [◄]

Nova Steel evolved from a $3 million, single-slitter Montreal operation that was founded in 1979 by D. Bryan Jones, Novamerican's president and CEO. Today it boasts 23 production and distribution centres throughout North America. As a publicly traded corporation (NAS-DAQ SYMBOL-TONS), annual sales exceed $400 million U.S. and the company's goal of $1 billion in sales isn't far off.

Nova has 10 locations throughout Central Canada and is the Canadian arm of Novamerican Steel Inc., a public corporation formed after Nova acquired American Steel and Aluminum back in 1996. A processor and distributor of carbon steel, stainless steel and aluminum products, Novamerican serves as an intermediary between primary metal producers and the manufacturers who require processed metal. These products and services benefit a broad base of more than 14,000 customers throughout Canada and the United States. Customers include general steel fabricators and manufacturers of automobiles, automotive parts, construction and agricultural equipment.

(right) The Nova professionals are an experienced, motivated team of engineers and technicians offering innovative ideas and a responsive attitude.

(below) Nova's state-of-the-art tube mill produces to the highest quality standards and guarantees just in time delivery.

Activity in the Ontario market began in 1982, with leased facilities on Industrial Road in Cambridge. Today their modern 50,000 square foot facility on Pinebush Road in Cambridge employs over 70 people and, more importantly, has become the springboard to a rapidly expanding Ontario market that generates more than $120 million a year.

As a flat-rolled service centre and manufacturer of tubing and specialized end products, the company's focus is on value-added processing to meet the diverse and specific needs of its many customers. The Ontario operations include a 42,000-square-foot tubing facility that was built in Mississauga in 1997 to meet the exploding demand for hydroformed tubing in the automotive industry, and a more recent $31-million 170,000 square foot production facility in Stoney Creek. These three facilities have firmly established the company as a leading processor of flat-rolled steel in Ontario

This focused and dynamic growth doesn't occur by chance but is a direct result of a company known for aggressive, visionary leadership. Key expansions, strategic acquisitions and heavy investment in equipment and manufacturing processes have all spearheaded Novamerican's success and its ever-increasing role as a value-added producer of steel-related products.

The company's product line is extensive and includes tubing, hot rolled, cold rolled and coated steel, plate, aluminum and stainless steels. Its value-added processes involve blanking, flame cutting, levelling, manufacturing, pickling, roll forming, shearing, slitting and tubing. In addition, its manufactured goods include excavator loader buckets, nails and nailers, racking and shelving systems and components for aboveground swimming pools. Indeed, the broad product lines and diverse customer base have allowed for unabated growth despite the ever-present vagaries of the steel-related marketplace.

Quality has also been a key factor in Nova's impressive growth. The company's quality control procedures have evolved to meet and even exceed the increasingly stringent quality assurance requirements of customers. Nova Ontario, which is QS 9000-certified, stresses quality control in all aspects of its products—from the time the material is ordered to actual processing and shipping. These controls and procedures involve periodic supplier audits, as well as rigorous inspection criteria. They ensure that the company never wavers from its firm vision to be a respected and competitive supplier of steel products and services through a commitment to superior customer satisfaction. Such a vision is enthusiastically embraced by Novamerican's 900 highly trained and dedicated employees who thrive in a culture that promotes teamwork.

Novamerican's formula for continuing growth and success will be to build on its proven track record of anticipating trends and making the necessary modifications to take advantage of new opportunities. Its current strategies revolve around four key industry trends: 1) growing customer demand for value and quality of products and services, 2) increased outsourcing of manufacturing processes by North American manufacturers, 3) the rising number of consolidations among major players within the industry, and 4) a shift by major customers to deal with fewer and larger suppliers.

As the industry has adopted a one-stop-shopping mentality,

Novamerican has vigilantly increased its value-added arsenal of products and services. For example, in their supply of pickled and oiled tubing, Nova controls the product through their very own pickler, slitter and tube mill. The ongoing quest for new value-added services will eventually allow the company to add other services and further broaden its appeal in the industry.

Key investments and acquisitions have well positioned Novamerican to respond to the increasing outsourcing needs of its customers. Indeed, it is ready to fill emerging market gaps and enhance its status in the industry. [■]

(above) With over 30,000 tons of inventory, Nova is committed to service the rapidly expanding Ontario market.

(left) Our newest processing centre has a 400,000 ton per year capacity pickling line with enhanced capabilities for a broader range of customer needs.

Although self propelled elevating work platforms were first used in the United States some 30 years ago, a thriving Guelph-based company can take much of the credit for their ever-increasing popularity.

The company is Skyjack Inc. established in Brampton in 1981 and relocated to Guelph in 1989, Skyjack has become a leading manufacturer of self-propelled scissor-type elevating work platforms. Using hydraulic powered arms that "scissor" upward and retract to a compact position, these lifts are attached to a self-propelled base which operates on electric or internal combustion power sources.

Increasingly regarded as a safe and economic alternative to scaffolding, Skyjack's quality products are now commonly used in a wide variety of elevated work settings, from the construction and maintenance of elevated roadways, bridges and tunnels to the repair of large aircraft.

Skyjack manufactures a complete line of scissor-type elevating products, boasting a variety of platform sizes and heights ranging from 15 to 50 feet.

Through its Skyjack Manufacturing Inc. subsidiary in Emmetsburg, Iowa, it also manufactures and distributes a wide range of push-around personnel lift models. With platform heights ranging from 6 to 40 feet, the push around models are ideal for use by one person in primarily indoor venues such as arenas, churches, schools and gymnasiums.

And through its Skyjack Equipment Inc. subsidiary in Atlantic, Iowa, the company also produces a line of self-propelled boom-type elevating platforms that enable safe and efficient access around obstructed areas.

Skyjack was founded by Wolf Haessler, the company's CEO. Back in 1969, Haessler, a mechanical engineer, co-founded a company called Haessler & De Way. Originally a designer and manufacturer of custom machinery for industrial customers throughout Canada and the United States, the company evolved into a manufacturer of special purpose machinery and equipment for packaging, food processing and material handling systems. Then, in 1978, while still producing these products, the Skyjack seeds were sown. That's when Haessler foresaw a growing demand for scissor-type elevated work platforms and envisioned their production using

Haessler & De Way's well-established skills and expertise.

Three years later, a prototype design was developed and Skyjack Inc. was born. In 1985, after Haessler was forced to wait out the recessionary climate of the early 80s, his fledgling company produced its first 100 scissor-type elevating platforms. They were ultimately sold to a major Toronto based equipment sales and rental firm. Skyjack was on its way.

Today, the company employs some 1100 people, sells products worldwide and boasts a market share approaching 20 per cent. Known for its aggressive pursuit of new and evolving markets, Skyjack now exports 90 per cent of the products it manufactures, mostly in the United States, Asia and Europe.

And the company continues to grow. By the end of 1998, for example, Skyjack had hired 100 additional employees in Guelph following the construction of a 150,000-square-foot manufacturing facility adjacent to its already formidable

Campbell Road headquarters. The facility now spans 350,000 square feet and employs 700 highly skilled and thoroughly trained people.

In addition to its Iowa subsidiaries, the company boasts a facility in Georgetown, Ontario, that houses the revitalized operations of Amador Aerials Inc. of Brampton and also produces one model of scissor lifts for the world market. Skyjack also boasts a service training centre in St. Charles, Illinois, a research and development facility in Wathena, Kansas, to assist in new product development, a research, development and light manufacturing facility in Loebau, Germany and a service, parts and product distribution centre in Mijdrecht, The Netherlands.

And despite the diverse roles these various facilities play in Skyjack's ongoing success, they are linked by a common denominator—an absolute obsession with quality and superior customer service.

The company makes its relationships with dealers and customers its number one priority. It devotes significant time, effort and resources to maintain and improve those relationships via committed service and the best possible levels of support. Consequently, it enjoys long-term relationships with the vast majority of its dealers and boasts a minuscule dealer turnover rate.

The company places heavy emphasis on research and development—almost $5 million in fiscal 1998—both to enhance the quality and efficiency of its lift devices and to develop the new product lines that will ensure ongoing growth.

Meanwhile, Skyjack management has created an all-pervasive culture in which its employees, recognized as the key to the company's ongoing success, enthusiastically embrace its dedication to quality and service. The non-unionized company invests heavily in employee training initiatives to provide the technical and management skills that keeps Skyjack a step ahead of the competition. Through its affiliation with area community colleges, the company encourages employees to enrol in apprenticeship programs, academic upgrading or other courses to enhance their careers with Skyjack. It also actively supports employees who wish to take on new challenges with the company or relocate to other facilities.

Certainly, Wolf Haessler has always adhered to the philosophy that employees should be rewarded and recognized for their contributions towards a company's success. Which is why Skyjack pays 15 per cent of pre-tax earnings as a bonus to its employees each quarter, why employees boasting long-term service are given generous options in the company and why Skyjack staff can take advantage of a long list of employee-related activities that implicitly say "thank you."

Not surprisingly, therefore, Skyjack's excellence and innovation have been recognized via a number of prestigious business and entrepreneurial awards, including the 1996 Ontario Entrepreneur of the Year award, the 1995 Canada Award for Excellence in the entrepreneur category, the 1995 Canada Export Award, 1995 Forbes Magazine recognition as one of the best small companies in the world, the 1994 Canadian Venture Capital Entrepreneur of the Year award and the 1994 Ontario Chamber of Commerce award for outstanding business achievement.

Certainly, such quality and innovation will enable the company to enhance its leadership role in the market it serves, a market where major growth is expected in the foreseeable future. As that growth occurs, as self-propelled lift devices gain increasing recognition for their advantages over traditional scaffolding and ladders, Skyjack is certainly well positioned to capitalize. [■]

That number has since grown to 16, and 90 to 95 per cent of RMS's products are now exported to countries such as India, Brazil, Mexico, Taiwan, Phillipines, Australia, Europe and the United States. More recently, the company has made formidable inroads into mainland China, where its sales have surpassed $17 million in the last two years alone.

Although the company's primary source of business remains the tire industry, officials here know all too well that a little flexibility can also go a long way. The lesson learned in the late 1970s, when RMS was almost forced to close its doors due to the enormous debt incurred by Uniroyal, its parent company at the time, hasn't been forgotten. RMS officials know the company would likely have succumbed had management not opted to break tradition and seek, for the first time, business over and above contracts secured by its parent company. Ultimately, RMS landed lucrative contracts with Ford, Chrysler and General Motors to produce transfer lines to machine automotive engine parts.

That flexibility remains a cornerstone of RMS's philosophy today. Its extensive team of innovative engineers and a complement of highly skilled employees who take to heart the motto—RMS pride: a tradition since 1917—have established a glowing reputation for their ability to design and produce a diverse range of high quality products, everything from tiny embossing dies weighing less than an ounce to huge structural assemblies of more than 80 tons.

Says Jack O'Donnell, it all boils down to what the customer wants. "We let the customers determine what product they want and we're small enough and flexible enough to be able to modify our products to fit their specific needs."

That philosophy enabled RMS's growth to proceed unabated during the recent recession.

More importantly, O'Donnell predicts RMS's customer service and flexibility will help the company adapt as the tire industry it has served admirably for the better part of a century continues to undergo dramatic change. [■]

RMS Corporation may not be bigger than the corporate Goliaths it competes with in the global market, but the company's affable, unabashedly confident president will tell you it is definitely better.

"We're good and we recognize we're good," Jack O'Donnell says of the Kitchener-based company which employs 110 people and has designed and manufactured industrial machinery for the tire industry since 1917. "I can tell you that once we get a customer, we have a customer for life."

In any case, RMS Corporation must be doing something right. With annual sales approaching $30 million worldwide, the company is coming off the two most successful years in its storied, 81-year history. And the foreseeable future appears equally promising.

The company has undergone numerous changes since its beginnings in an 18,000-square-foot machine shop that served as a division of Dominion Tire Co. Ltd. Its state-of-the-art headquarters, emblazoned with a Canadian flag alongside the company logo, has grown to more than 60,000 square feet since then. It has operated under a variety of parent companies, including the Uniroyal Tire Co., Uniroyal-Goodrich and Michelin.

The most significant change in the company's long history transpired in 1993, when O'Donnell, with his partner Michael O'Reilly and a group of employee investors, purchased RMS's assets from Michelin.

The now locally owned and operated company hasn't looked back. At the time of the purchase, for instance, RMS's global presence outside of North America consisted of a lone sales agent in South Korea.

LIBERTY LINEHAUL

At the back entrance of Liberty Linehaul Inc.'s terminal near Cambridge, a small sign bears the simple, hand-scrawled message, "Welcome home."

A token gesture? Not to the drivers and employees who regularly pass through the entranceway of this award-winning, specialized freight carrier. To them, the message provides further evidence of the steps their company has taken to create their enviable work environment. Because in this day and age of corporate rationalizations and bottom line results, Liberty is refreshing proof that the creation of a genuine family-like work setting can go hand in hand with the outstanding customer service that spawns success. So when a company driver who happened to be on the road near Dallas learned that his mother had become desperately ill, he was told to leave his rig there and fly home immediately. The company paid for the flight. Such gestures, commonplace here, go hand in hand with above-average compensation packages. With an extensive employee assistance program offering everything from family counselling to legal advice. With a gleaming maintenance record to enhance driver safety. With comprehensive training programs to help employees be the best they can be. And with liberal recognition for exemplary service, either in the form of monetary rewards or promotion. In fact, virtually all of the company's managers have risen through the ranks internally.

The result? Liberty not only has among the lowest employee turnover rates in the industry but its employees also routinely demonstrate their willingness to go the extra mile. And if the bottom line is what you're after, Liberty's revenue-to-truck ratio also ranks among the best in the industry. "You care about your employees and they'll care about your customers; it's that simple," says Brian Taylor, the company's vice-president.

Liberty, one of a handful of Ontario companies to have achieved "premium carrier" status, eschews head-on competition with larger trucking firms. Its focus is a niche market—specialized, high-level service tailored to the individual requirements of customers. Its air-ride trucks, equipped with satel-

lite messaging, will deliver full or less than full loads. It has the specialized equipment and expertise to take on the most fragile, high value items that need to reach their destination unscathed within a specific window of time. And whether the freight is a small, delicately-balanced, $180,000 gadget for the space shuttle, or the one-of-a-kind sports car used in the movie *Back to the Future*, the company fulfils its mandate with remarkable consistency.

Living up to its billing as "Canada's Elite Fleet," Liberty's glowing reputation has spawned steady growth since its inception in 1987. Four trucks and 12 employees have grown to 130 employees and 45 trucks that deliver their delicate wares throughout North America. Demand is so great, Taylor says the company could have chosen to grow even more rapidly. But it has maintained a slow, steady course in order to retain its flexibility and superior level of service. Besides, Taylor will tell you he never tires of the steady stream of letters he receives from satisfied customers eager to extol the exemplary efforts of a company driver and/or staff member. "I've always said the goal is to be the best trucking company in Canada," he says. "Hopefully, it makes money. But the important thing is to be the very best we can be." [◼]

CHICOPEE MANUFACTURING LIMITED

Thanks to its reputation for outstanding precision and quality, Kitchener's Chicopee Manufacturing Limited continues its ascension to exciting new heights.

Certainly, it's hard to envision that this privately held Canadian company, established in 1953 as W.R. Elliott Limited, originally produced an assortment of steel products that included little red wagons.

These days, each Boeing 737 that soars majestically into the horizon takes a piece of Chicopee along for the ride. That's because this thriving company, which officially took on the Chicopee name in 1975, has become a top producer of precision machined components and sub assemblies, the vast majority of which is earmarked for the ever-evolving aerospace industry.

Within its 120,000-square-foot facility, 200 highly skilled employees use state-of-the-art technology and machinery to produce a wide variety of steel products, including bulkheads, frames, leading edge details, flap tracks and engine mount structures that withstand the most rigorous specifications and expectations of global aeronautical giants like Boeing and Bombardier.

Not that some of the company's products aren't a bit more grounded as well. Among Chicopee's other customers is General Motors of Canada Limited, for whom the company produces custom gear cases for diesel engines.

In any case, the company's evolution has coincided with its ever-growing and indisputable expertise in the use of high strength steels, titanium and a variety of aluminum alloys. That expertise continues to enable the company, which was purchased in early 1998 by the Magellan Aerospace Corporation, to tackle a wide range of machining challenges and meet the stringent, ever-changing specifications of its customers.

As a result, Chicopee, now widely recognized across North America as a leader in the field of aeronautical manufacturing, has watched its overall sales figures more than double during the last three years.

But although Chicopee's expertise is the initial attraction for prospective customers, company officials will tell you it's an absolute dedication to quality, an attitude that pervades this operation from the shop floor to its executive offices, that has helped ensure ongoing customer loyalty. Quite simply, this ISO 9002 company has a passion for customer service, so much so that it stands ever ready to solve a customer's unique needs and problems, even if the ultimate solution involves modifications to its product or the way things are done.

At the same time, Chicopee works diligently to maintain some of the highest quality control standards in the industry. Among other things, it has embraced the Total Quality Improvement philosophy and has incorporated Statistical Process Control into its highly efficient production system.

Its quality control procedures initially require an inspection of every operation, as well as a 100 per cent final inspection of all critical dimensions to ensure that reverse traceability of all materials, parts and processes is guaranteed.

In a further effort to meet its commitment to quality, Chicopee also possesses in-house capabilities to provide various types of non-destructive testing.

The bottom line? Chicopee Manufacturing Limited and its highly skilled employees are deservedly proud of their products and reputation.

But that pride, however justified, will not breed complacency. Instead, a number of peer-driven initiatives ensure Chicopee's never-ending drive for the continuous improvement to help the company maintain its secure foothold at the forefront of its industry. ◖◗

Creation of a part program for a CNC machine on a CAD/CAM system.

Machining of a precision component on a state-of-the-art horizontal machining centre.

KAPPELER MASONRY

For a highly successful businessman, Gerhard "Dick" Kappeler's perspective on profitability seems rather extraordinary in these bottom-line-driven times.

"I'd rather lose financially on a project than [cut corners] and lose a customer," the affable president of Waterloo's Kappeler Masonry (Conestogo) Ltd. will tell you matter-of-factly. "Before profit comes quality workmanship and a satisfied customer."

In any case, Kappeler's business philosophy has certainly paid off. Unlike many established masonry companies that succumbed to the building industry's nosedive of the early 1990s, Kappeler Masonry has continued to flourish and build on its exceptional reputation.

Some 100 employees, including some of the finest craftsmen in the industry, now ply their skills for the family-owned-and-operated company that Kappeler and his wife, Wanda, launched more than 30 years ago in an east-end Kitchener apartment. What's more, the company recently moved into a brand new 10,000-square-foot facility a mere stone's throw from the renowned St. Jacobs Farmers' Market. Self-designed and self-built, the building stands with the many Kappeler projects—institutional, industrial, commercial and historical restoration—showcasing the company's unequivocal trademark of quality workmanship.

In fact, Kappeler Masonry, whose market now encompasses most of Southern Ontario, hasn't spent so much as a dime on advertising during its proud history. Instead, the company lets its performance do the talking, be it the extensive restoration of the historic Dominion Building in downtown London or the exquisite renovation of Stratford's city hall. As a company spearheaded by top-notch specialists in structural stonework, granite facing, limestone facing and both brick and block-work, Kappeler Masonry is a company that has been built solely on its performance and the word-of-mouth recommendations of a long line of truly satisfied customers.

Its president, an accomplished stonemason by trade, wouldn't have it any other way. Because notwithstanding his obvious prowess as an entrepreneur, Kappeler, who has honed

his skills from the time he was a wide-eyed 14-year-old in his native Germany, is first and foremost a craftsman. Like the painter who applies his or her unique strokes to canvas, so too does he and his highly skilled personnel leave their singularly distinctive legacies in each of the always challenging projects they tackle.

Among Kappeler's chief concerns, however, is that North America's affinity for stonework is fast becoming a lost art, that for various reasons the skilled masons of yesteryear declined to pass their knowledge on to subsequent generations. Indeed, the bulk of Kappeler Masonry's craftsmen hail from countries such as Germany and Scotland, where stone continues to be revered as a flexible, sturdy building material promising a lifespan of several generations.

One of Kappeler Masonry's goals, therefore, is to further its founder's dream.

"I'm very proud of what I've learned over the years," Kappeler says. " I want to leave my knowledge behind so that it can be passed on to young people who will continue the trade in future generations."

The process has already begun. Kappeler's sons, Gary and Dan, have worked their way through the ranks of the company and have supervised a number of major projects in preparation for the day they take over the business and build upon their parents' proud legacy. The company has also taken on a number of young, eager Canadians who are learning the skills of the trade while working alongside Kappeler Masonry's vastly experienced personnel.

In the meantime, it's a safe bet that Kappeler Masonry will continue to thrive, thanks to its deeply embedded quality-before-profit doctrine. [■]

(Left) Dick Kappeler.

(Top) Ingersol Public Library.

Dominion Building Restoration.

CHAPTER TEN

Business Community 10

Photo by Mike Grandmaison

ENGEL CANADA, INC.

On a recent midweek afternoon, a handful of rapt employees flank a boardroom table strewn with scribbled notes and technical specifications.

Their discussion revolves around a customer's rather daunting request for a machine customized to possess higher-than-standard speed capabilities.

A formidable and as-yet-untried challenge to be sure. But the phrase "we can't" is not uttered here. Instead, these employees, most of whom have accepted and overcome more than their share of challenges in the past, emerge from this meeting determined to find a way.

And so it is a rather typical day at Guelph's Engel Canada Inc., a company that has become a world leader in the design and manufacture of leading edge injection molding machines for producers of plastic and a host of other material products and parts.

Indeed, such meetings are anything but an oddity at Engel, a company whose astounding success and staggering growth boils down to two words—added value. Time and time again, the company has met such challenges head-on. Time and time again, it has applied its vast technological resources, not to mention the expertise of some of the top engineers in the industry, to develop the innovative solutions sought by its customers, many of whom enjoy Fortune 500 status. In fact, some 80 per cent of the machines produced at the state-of-the-art Guelph plant, which also serves as headquarters for Engel North America, leave here with some degree of customization.

"Over the years we have learned to be very flexible when it comes to our customers' specifications," explains Karl Pieper, the company's president. "We have found a niche in the industry. That niche is added value."

While some of its major competitors produce lower cost 'off-the-shelf' injection molding machines, Pieper says Engel has opted to set itself apart by eschewing a "we can't" or "we won't" attitude in order to develop the application-specific options that help their loyal customers gain an edge in an ever-competitive global marketplace. The company's reputation has been built on its proven ability to develop optional molding processes and technologies that improve quality and precision while minimizing manufacturing costs.

The company holds the patent, for instance, on the tieberless clamp, an innovation that gives injection molders a decided competitive advantage because it allows them to mount a larger mold in a smaller machine and, in the process, significantly reduce their fixed operating costs.

The bottom line is that many of the most demanding products on the market today, from under-the-hood components in the automotive industry, to computers, toys, personal care products, medical components and packaging, are produced on Engel injection molding machines.

For the record, Engel is an Austrian-based, family-owned business founded in 1945 by Ludwig Engel. Guelph's Engel Canada was formed 30 years later, in 1975, as a sales and service subsidiary boasting three employees who operated out of cramped, rented facilities. In 1977, the company moved to its own 30,000-square-foot plant on its current Elmira Road site. Ever since, the company has enjoyed virtually unabated growth. Three major expansions later, the Guelph facility now occupies more than 240,000 square feet, boasts more than 550 employees, and lays claim to a growth rate that has averaged about 35 per cent over the last four years.

The main Guelph plant, which accommodates all development, engineering, machining of parts, assembly, and the writing of software, builds smaller injection molding machines ranging from 40 to 500 tons. An adjacent 30,000-square-foot facility houses the production of Engel's complete line of automation technology for North America, including its integrated, high-speed robots. Meanwhile, a York, Pennsylvania, subsidiary, Engel Machinery Inc., produces injection molding machines of 500 tons and more. Combined, the three entities surpassed sales of $210 million last year.

In every sense of the word, Engel, which has installed more than 30,000 machines in over 80 countries, is an aggressive global company. Some 80 per cent of Engel Canada's products, for example, are exported to the United States, Mexico, the Caribbean and South America. But despite its strong global presence, Engel's operations continue to adhere to the traditional family values on which lasting relationships are built—trust, dependability, reliability and commitment to service.

The result is both an intensely loyal customer base and a minuscule

employee turnover rate that allows the company to constantly enhance its product expertise.

In fact, Engel boasts some of the most highly skilled, experienced and dedicated employees in the industry. It is a company which believes in the philosophy of promoting from within, a company that fosters a deep commitment to craftmanship and encourages continuous personal development at all levels through a variety of training programs and government recognized apprenticeship initiatives. Wherever possible, theoretical practice is fortified through hands-on training in modern machine and automation laboratories. And through active employee associations, social committees, as well as safety and quality circles, Engel and its employees continue to nurture a strong, tight-knit partnership through genuine communication.

Small wonder, Engel Canada, a strong corporate citizen, was recently named as a recipient of the Ontario Chamber of Commerce's Outstanding Business Achievement Award.

In the meantime, demand continues to grow, and expansion is imminent once again. The company currently builds about 600 machines a year at the Guelph plant, as well as

about 150 robots. Demand is such that the company wants to build as many as 750 machines in Guelph in the foreseeable future in addition to between 250 and 300 robots.

To accommodate such stepped-up production, plans are being developed for yet another massive addition to the Guelph facility within the next year or two. That expansion will also lead to the creation of many more jobs for this already burgeoning area.

In many ways, Engel serves as a striking example to other companies trying to find a formula for success.

In Engel, such enterprises will discover that real success is still achievable through the time-honoured principles of old-fashioned hard work, traditional values embracing such characteristics as loyalty and dependability, and a genuine concern for the individual needs and requirements of the customer. [■]

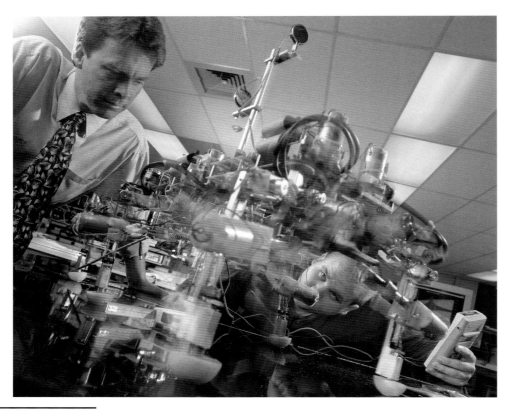

Waterloo's Faculty of Engineering is home to strong basic and applied research programs.

Anyone doubting the exemplary status of the University of Waterloo's engineering faculty may want to have a conversation or two with the employers who covet its graduates.

They would confront representatives of some of Canada's major high-tech industries who would readily acknowledge that graduates from UW's founding faculty are in such demand that the recruitment process begins in earnest when these students are still in their initial year of study.

Which isn't bad for a faculty whose rather daring launch 42 years ago drew plenty of scorn from the country's academic establishment.

That was back in 1957. A group of leading Kitchener-Waterloo industrialists decided the area was ripe for an institution that could provide relevant technical education, a school that could guarantee the region's businesses a steady stream of qualified engineers.

So they decided to found a university, which then hired a group of young, brash and innovative faculty members and introduced Canada's first-ever co-operative system of education.

Scorn gave way to profound admiration long ago.

Engineering is Waterloo's founding faculty, the first to employ UW's innovative co-operative education program.

After all, the faculty now boasts some 3,400 undergraduate and 600 graduate students, and accepts 750 first-year students each year. Which happens to make it the largest engineering faculty in the country.

Certainly, the sky's-the-limit innovative spirit that carried the faculty in its initial stages has continued to live on. Back in the mid-'70s, for instance, faculty officials sensed computers would one day play an integral role in electrical engineering. So, in 1978, they started a computer science option. Six years later, demand for the program was so great the faculty launched the country's first computer engineering degree program. Today, it is the largest, most respected program of its type in the country.

Indeed, UW's engineering faculty has garnered international acclaim during its history, both for the impressive academic credentials of its students and faculty members, and the program that attracts them.

Its co-op program, among the world's largest, has earned an enviable reputation. Students who participate in the co-op program can expect two things—that they will earn good co-op salaries to help ease the financial burden of their university education, and that they will leave school armed with highly relevant, cutting-edge engineering experience.

Both the quality of the jobs these students land during their co-op work terms and the financial compensation they receive are second to none. On any given day you'll find co-op students involved in prestigious placements throughout North America or participating in once-in-a-lifetime exchange opportunities in countries throughout Europe and Asia.

A number of successful companies lining a busy industrial corridor along Highway 401 will also tell you that they have become quite dependent on the engineering faculty's co-op students, whose duties can range from computer software design to conducting feasibility studies. And the leaders of major corporations, such as Nortel, will vouch for the fact that many of their products have been built on the contributions of UW engineering co-op students.

So relevant is the experience these students receive that a host of area companies have been launched by engineering students who are still in their third year of study. Many of these companies also hire first-year students for co-op placements and graduates.

UW engineering students are highly prepared for the placements they receive, thanks to a team of top-notch professors and a program where the individual success of its students borders on an obsession. In fact, the faculty boasts the lowest failure rate in the country. And while much of that speaks to the high levels of intelligence of those who study here, it is also testimony to the measures the faculty has taken to identify, correct and eradicate roadblocks to a student's success. It's referred to as "the life vest" here. It involves a number of tests and monitors that gauge first-year students' proficiency in areas such as English and math preparedness. For those encountering academic difficulty, the faculty offers various kinds of help to clear a student's path to ultimate success.

But the engineering faculty contributes more to the community it serves than just its 20,000 alumni. In addition to generating innovative research projects and 20,000 alumni world-wide, UW's engineering faculty has also spawned numerous spin-off enterprises, many of them located close to the university. Employing thousands, these businesses contribute tens of millions of dollars to the local economy each year.

And that's merely the first wave. Dr. Sujeet Chaudhuri, the faculty's dean, predicts that another wave of spin-off companies is imminent. And given the depth and diversity of research currently being conducted here, Chaudhuri believes that next wave will be even more pronounced.

Meanwhile, UW's engineering students have earned a substantial reputation for their level of maturity and community responsibility. For the last 25 years, for instance, engineering students have participated in the annual "bus push" (it's actually a bus pull) to raise money for the area's Big Sisters Association. The event has become the organization's largest fundraiser.

Students here also reach out to the community by running an annual summer camp called ESQ—Engineering Science Quest—in which youngsters from Grade 4 through to Grade 12 spend a week on campus to use the various facilities, engage in fun experiments and enjoy numerous athletic and recreational pursuits. The program was launched several years ago

with 200 students. Today, it attracts more than 900 annually.

What's more, engineering and science students are looking for ways to raise money so that they can make the program even more accessible to young people confronting serious financial limitations.

And in 1991 students pioneered the notion of a student endowment fund to ensure ongoing improvements in teaching facilities and equipment for undergraduate students. Called WEEF (Waterloo Engineering Endowment Foundation), more than 70 per cent of all engineering students contribute at least $75 a term to this fund, which has surpassed $3 million. Officials expect the fund to surpass $6 million in the next five years, which makes it one of the largest student-run endowment funds in the country.

In short, UW's engineering faculty has more than justified

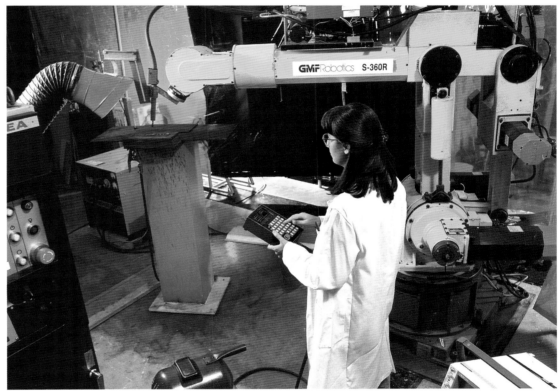

the vision of the early industrialists who founded it. Through innovation, an obsessive pursuit of excellence and an ongoing desire to build upon the formidable momentum it has achieved, it continues to take those original expectations and stretch them to once unimaginable heights. [■]

A Bachelor of Applied Science from Waterloo is one of the most valuable and sought-after engineering degrees in the world.

CANADA'S TECHNOLOGY TRIANGLE

(ECONOMIC DEVELOPMENT IN CANADA'S TECHNOLOGY TRIANGLE INC.)

Photo by Mike Grandmaison.

Ask most locals to define Canada's Technology Triangle (CTT) and they'll likely refer to an incredibly rich, diverse geographic area situated in the midst of Canada's business and industrial heartland. Now meet the other CTT, the unique partnership that seeks to ensure the continuing economic development of that geographic region. Originally created as an informal partnership of municipalities in 1987, the organization has evolved to the point of being incorporated in 1999 under the name 'Economic Development in Canada's Technology Triangle Inc.'

Throughout its history, this coalition of the area's municipalities, business community, educational institutions and a range of affiliate organizations has had a profound impact. Not only does the organization provide the support and expertise to help existing area businesses strengthen their toehold in an increasingly globalized marketplace, but it is working diligently to attract outside businesses eyeing either expansion or relocation here.

Canada's Technology Triangle has plenty to work with. The area it serves includes the five vibrant municipalities of Cambridge, Guelph, Kitchener, Waterloo and the Regional Municipality of Waterloo – some

500,000 people in all and a skilled labour force of more than 260,000.

Here, a pronounced entrepreneurial spirit and buoyant, expanding economy share the spotlight with some of the richest and most productive farmland in Ontario, not to mention traditional farmers' markets, 11 indoor and 15 outdoor swimming pools, 24 hockey arenas, 18 golf courses, an active ski area and with nine malls, 61 factory outlets and several markets, enough shopping variety to please just about everyone. All this in an area whose unemployment rates have traditionally remained at levels significantly lower than the national and provincial averages.

Location is one key to the area's bustling economy. The area is situated within an hour's drive of the city of Toronto and is also positioned to service more than 120 million people who are located within a day's drive. The area's network of strategically placed business and industrial parks is closely linked to the major thoroughfares, including rail and air, that provide ready access to both the densely populated southern Ontario and northeastern United States markets.

Canada's Technology Triangle has fashioned an exemplary history of business achievement, featuring a diverse range of enterprises that has allowed it to roll with any recessionary punches to come its way. The gross domestic product of the more than 14,000 businesses which thrive in this relatively small geographic area matches that of the entire province of

New Brunswick and exceeds the combined output of Prince Edward Island, Newfoundland, Yukon and the Northwest Territories.

In addition to CTT's enterprises in sectors such as the automotive industry, traditional manufacturing and a solid core of financial services, the area also finds itself on the leading edge of technological research and development. In recent years, a rapidly growing number of companies have emerged to produce and supply products to a burgeoning high-tech sector. Research and subsequent innovations in laser technology, micro-electronics, agri-food, biotech research and computer-related design, manufacturing and software have been key components to a local economy whose rate of growth continues to outpace the provincial average.

The vibrancy and dynamics of CTT have been aided by the presence and involvement of four world-class educational institutions including three major universities—Guelph, Waterloo and Wilfrid Laurier – as well as Conestoga College of Applied Arts and Technology. While these institutions boast a long history of providing the training and essential education for an ongoing supply of highly skilled labour, they have also played a major role in helping to incubate and develop many of the thriving enterprises in existence today. At the same time, these academic institutions continue to provide invaluable support to the private sector in terms of research, creativity, innovation studies and world-class computer-related expertise.

Canada's Technology Triangle has a significant presence as an economic development engine. It has a strong influence in bringing all the forces and the various partners together to work towards a common goal and help move the economy in the area forward. In addition to the municipalities, educational institutions and the Chambers of Commerce, CTT's supporting partners include selected business-related organizations which offer specific services and expertise.

The Economic Development Corporation is the single, best information resource for companies assessing the benefits of establishing or expanding a presence in the area thanks to a support group that will go the extra mile and work closely with a company's search team to answer questions, compile reports and

supply essential data.

For search teams making their initial visit to the area, The Economic Development Corporation provides an executive briefing to highlight the area's geography, economy and demographics. It also provides a tour of the area that focuses on prospective sites, buildings, development centres and other points of interest. The organization will even provide assistance with travel and accommodation.

Companies considering a move to Canada's Technology Triangle can readily access an up to date inventory of available business and industrial sites. The Economic Development Corporation will also work closely with company officials to identify and arrange confidential appointments with the area's professionals and community leaders, thereby ensuring an efficient and thorough fact finding visit.

In short, Canada's Technology Triangle is open for business. Our proud tradition of excellence combined with the dedicated and expert support that CTT provides will ensure the area's strong presence and continued growth in the new economy. [◄]

(below) *Photo by Mike Grandmaison.*

CAMBRIDGE CHAMBER OF COMMERCE

"Welcome to Cambridge! The Cambridge Chamber of Commerce has operated the Cambridge Visitor & Convention Bureau on behalf of the City of Cambridge since 1981. We would be pleased to help you with your plans for a conference, business trip or family visit to our community."

Economically speaking, the city of Cambridge has fared pretty well in recent years.

Certainly, its proximity to Toronto and an abundance of serviceable industrial land adjacent to major arteries like Highway 401 are major factors. But this city also enjoys a positive, buoyant business climate that continues to attract a spate of new companies and helps persuade existing firms to expand.

For that, the Cambridge Chamber of Commerce, some 900 members strong, can accept much of the credit. Since forming in 1973 to coincide with the amalgamation of the former municipalities of Galt, Preston and Hespeler, the organization has more than earned its billing as the voice of the city's business community.

Whether vigorously promoting Cambridge (the organization also operates the city's Visitor and Convention Bureau), helping to form legislative policy, or lobbying various levels of government on behalf of its membership, the Chamber is widely recognized as a key partner in Cambridge's impressive economic development.

And as the well-known television commercial suggests, membership has its advantages. So much so that the organization has attracted 150 new members in the last 18 months alone.

Among other things, those members, whether corporate giants like Toyota or smaller owner/operator enterprises, are attracted by the networking opportunities and information exchange their membership affords them. After all, the Chamber is known for the many informal events it offers so that members can keep abreast of new developments while fortifying their crucial, word-of-mouth presence in the community.

The indisputable backbone of this vibrant organization, however, is its core of volunteers. The Chamber's seven staff members are supported by more than 100 volunteers, many of them recognized leaders in the local business community.

These volunteers lend their experience, creativity, expertise and passion to a number of standing committees ranging from advocacy to education to business resources. They help produce a variety of newsletters and pamphlets

to keep members informed of new laws, trends and developments.

And with an eye to the business climate of the future, they also help spearhead a number of initiatives geared towards youth. Among them is a highly successful mentoring program in which business volunteers work one-on-one with high school students dangerously close to dropping out.

And speaking of the future... the Chamber is about to leave its currently cramped quarters in the former town of Preston's Allan Reuter Centre behind. By the year 2000, the organization is expected to move into a new, much larger facility appropriately dubbed The Gateway.

The Gateway is a joint venture with the City of Cambridge. An 8,000-square-foot facility, twice the Chamber's current size, it will be ideally located at the southwest corner of Highways 401 and 24, one of Cambridge's predominant entrances. Fund-raising is proceeding in earnest for the $1-million project.

The new facility will allow the organization to host more events and activities on site, accommodate an extensive display area to better promote Cambridge's services and attractions, and house a comprehensive resource centre for smaller and start-up businesses.

Sam Purdy, the Chamber's hardworking Chair of the Board of Directors, says The Gateway will provide "a great face forward" for the city and significantly enhance the Chamber's already formidable support of Cambridge's thriving business community. [◾]

The Cambridge Chamber of Commerce offers the business community many opportunities to network and learn—from plant tours to seminars, to name but a few.

SIMS CLEMENT EASTMAN

Way back in 1858, in a village then known as Berlin, Ward Hamilton Bowlby founded a law firm.

And while it's true he entered the enterprise with high expectations, he would certainly have been hard-pressed to predict that his fledgling firm, founded on the fundamental tenet of committed service, would still be going strong some 140 years later.

Much has transpired since then. Edwin Perry Clement, the son of a travelling Methodist clergyman, would join Bowlby 13 years later, the first of several generations of Clements to do so. Berlin would be renamed Kitchener in 1916. The firm would grow through numerous partners and name changes. Today, Sims Clement Eastman is the area's largest locally owned law firm.

Located in spacious, art-decorated and antique-adorned quarters on the sixth, seventh and eighth floors of the building that once housed Kitchener's city hall, Sims Clement Eastman is a general service firm boasting 28 lawyers, 20 partners, eight associates, a second-to-none reputation, and an inextricable bond with the local community.

Thanks to a philosophy embracing the notion that dedicated client and community service go hand in hand, the firm lays claim to a long line of partners and lawyers who have made profound contributions to the area. Over the years it has produced mayors, city councillors, and a long line of individuals who have lent their time, talents and expertise to various community and governing bodies and charitable organizations. The tradition continues today as the firm's community-minded partners volunteer their time in endeavours ranging from homes for pregnant teens to Boy Scout organizations.

The firm's commitment to service has enabled it to enjoy unabated growth. The firm also has grown with a number of long-term clients. Those clients include the likes of major family-owned corporations such as Kaufman Footwear, Dare Foods, Electrohome, Economical Insurance and J.M. Schneider's—century-old companies who have referred and trusted their legal needs to Sims Clement Eastman for decades.

While the firm is steeped in proud tradition, it also continues to keep pace with the rapid changes necessary to maintain, and improve, its well-earned reputation for excellence.

To better serve the area's burgeoning high-tech industry and its global concerns, Sims Clement Eastman recently

formed a preferred alliance with a large Toronto national and international firm known for its expertise in this and other specialized areas of law. Sims Clement Eastman now has immediate access to the information it needs to provide quick and efficient legal service to its growing number of high-tech clients.

Continuing education is also an integral aspect of Sims Clement Eastman's philosophy. Lawyers who work here are strongly encouraged to keep abreast of changes in the law and upgrade their skills accordingly.

Practice Groups formed according to the specific areas of law they practice meet regularly to discuss new developments and devise new ways of serving their clients. At the same time, strategic planning retreats are a regular event here, and the search for new opportunities is ongoing. It goes without saying that the firm has also kept pace with the leading edge technology.

Simply put, Sims Clement Eastman has perfected a formula that would make Ward Hamilton Bowlby proud. Combining tradition and old-fashioned service with an openness to change, that formula will continue to drive the firm's success as it enters the new millennium. ◖▶

former chamber presidents, it was this very organization that spearheaded the creation of the region's two world-class universities.

That's not all. The chamber also helped launch Junior Achievement in Kitchener-Waterloo. It founded K-W Oktoberfest, North America's largest Bavarian festival. And it established both the Sounds of Summer, an annual showcase of some of the country's top musical talent, and the Busker's Festival, which each year highlights the bizarre talents and unpredictable shenanigans of some of Canada's top street performers.

But don't think this organization is content to rest on its laurels, however impressive they might be. Spearheaded by more than 400 volunteers, many of whom comprise the business elite of the area, the organization's efforts to bolster Kitchener-Waterloo's already buoyant business climate never stop.

As a result, the chamber now boasts over 100 benefits to its growing list of members. Among other things, the chamber offers its members a host of opportunities for networking and the exchange of ideas. Through a variety of special events, an extensive membership roster and free link-up to a substantial website, members have ample opportunity to significantly increase their visibility. Enterprises can take advantage of competitive group insurance packages. And a litany of workshops and seminars allow company representatives to hone their management skills or enhance personal and professional growth. The Chamber also serves the community through provision of tourism services and partners with the cities of Kitchener and Waterloo in tourism development to boost economic growth.

Of course, the chamber continues to effectively represent the concerns of its members to all levels of government on key issues ranging from taxation to transportation, economic development to health care. It played a significant role, for example, in recent local government tax reforms. And its current undertakings include the improvement of Waterloo Region's health care infrastructure. Consequently, the chamber has become the leading player in the vigorous efforts to attract much-needed physicians to the area.

Given its impressive track record, few would question the prominent role played by The Chamber of Commerce of Kitchener & Waterloo in the growth and prosperity of the vibrant community it serves.

Even the most cursory examination of this organization's long, distinguished history clearly indicates that the chamber's motto—"serving business in Kitchener-Waterloo and acting as its voice in the betterment of the community"—has proven to be so much more than a collection of hollow words.

Founded in 1886, the organization boasts a membership of some 1,600 companies which represent more than 44,000 employees, making it the second largest chamber of commerce in Ontario. It has played a key role in attracting numerous major businesses and industries to the area. And its tireless efforts to create an atmosphere conducive to business and commercial prosperity are well-documented.

Not as well known, perhaps, is the chamber's passionate belief in the inextricable link between business and community well-being. Based on that unwavering conviction, the chamber has played a leading role throughout a long list of major community developments over the years.

It was the chamber, for instance, that helped bring the railways here. It was the chamber that played a leading role in the ultimate construction of the area's expressway. And as evidenced by the many faculty buildings bearing the names of

Simply put, The Chamber of Commerce of Kitchener & Waterloo's vision is paved by the single-most important lesson it has learned during its remarkable history—that business prosperity and the community's quality of life must continue to walk hand-in-hand. [■]

GUELPH CHAMBER OF COMMERCE

When it comes to organizations boasting lengthy histories, Guelph's Chamber of Commerce need not take a backseat to anyone.

Its roots date back to 1827 when, a mere four months after the founding of this community, the Guelph Board of Commerce was launched to help stimulate economic growth.

The organization, renamed the Guelph Chamber of Commerce in 1919, has served as an influential voice of business for this bustling community ever since.

Boasting some 625 member organizations that encompass more than 1,000 representatives, the Chamber has been a key catalyst for the Royal City's economic growth and ongoing prosperity.

A dynamic and flexible organization ever ready to respond to its members' existing and emerging needs, the Chamber continues to forge strong links with a large number of community partners. Representatives from the City of Guelph, the University of Guelph, the public and separate school boards, the healthcare community, and a wide array of public and private sector organizations help drive a long list of vital Chamber committees and initiatives resulting in a second-to-none business climate.

Indeed, Chamber committees, which include industrial, environmental, education and government liaison, are spearheaded by a dedicated core of some 200 volunteers, many of them representing the who's who of the local business community.

As a result, the Chamber, which is affiliated with both the Ontario and Canadian Chambers of Commerce, has repeatedly proven itself as a powerful lobby in the business community's dealings with local, provincial and federal governments. Certainly, no other organization in Guelph can boast the Chamber's collective strength when dealing with the issues that affect business.

In addition, its influence has played a vital role in other aspects of this community. In 1989, for example, the Chamber, recognizing the inextricable link between a strong community and a healthy business climate, spearheaded a major fundraising drive to raise more than $12 million towards the redevelopment of Guelph's hospitals.

Certainly, no organization offers the networking and business visibility opportunities that the Guelph Chamber of Commerce can offer its members. Its programs include Business After 5, Networking Breakfast, Education Forum and

Lunch and Learn. Its special events include Outlook, held annually to examine the anticipated economic trends of the coming year, the three-year-old Guelph Quality Awards, which reward the exemplary continuous quality improvement practices of local businesses, and a highly popular annual golf tournament. Combined, these programs and events provide members with ample access to new business contacts and allow them to keep abreast of the latest business trends, practices and issues.

Membership has other advantages. In deference to its many members representing smaller businesses, the Chamber provides a number of specially-designed products and services, including low cost group insurance packages, a mentoring program called ViaSource and a natural gas discount program.

As for the future, the Chamber's already formidable clout in the community can only be enhanced, thanks to a current drive to increase its membership to 1,000 within the next three years.

Certainly, the Chamber's ability to meet the ever changing needs of business ensures its ongoing vitality as the organization continues to build on the vision of its founders more than 170 years ago. ◖◗

Photo by Mike Grandmaison

CHAPTER ELEVEN

Hospitality

11

Photo by Mike Grandmaison

Four Points by Sheraton.

In terms of size, a city such as Kitchener can hardly be compared to the Torontos of the world.

But if you happen to be a Kitchener hotel hoping to target the area's corporate market, it pays to offer the amenities and level of service such clientele have come to expect in more cosmopolitan cities.

At least that's the philosophy at Kitchener's Four Points by Sheraton Hotel, one which continues to drive its ever-growing success in a fiercely competitive industry.

"There are two major keys to the success we've had here," says Kelly McCauley, the upscale, full-service hotel's General Manager. "There is a service culture here that keeps guests happy, and we offer high quality amenities at mid-market prices. That's the reality of the hospitality industry today. People want value and there's an obvious demand for a high end, up-to-date product."

The Four Points Sheraton is owned by the Vancouver-based Canadian Hotel Income Properties Real Estate Investment Trust, CHIP REIT, (HOT.un:TSE) Canada's first hotel real estate investment trust and is managed by CHIP Hospitality, the REIT's hotel management division. CHIP Hospitality is also one of Canada's top five hotel management companies in terms of rooms available.

The hotel offers 200 rooms (15 suites), 13,000 square feet of meeting space on its convention level and dining facilities such as the 105 Deli & Bistro with its unique, deli and bistro cuisine. By December 1999 The Four Points Sheraton will have also completed $2 million in up-grades to guest rooms and public areas.

One of the modern and spacious rooms.

Fully Equipped Meeting Rooms

With its primary target market in mind, the hotel's meeting rooms come equipped with such key features as television and telephone outlets, individually controlled heating and air conditioning and ready access to state-of-the-art audio-visual equipment. Photocopy, secretarial and fax services are also readily available at a nominal fee.

Combine all these services with the hotel's ability to cater to the diverse needs of groups from 6 to 600, and it's hardly surprising that the Four Points Sheraton's corporate business—everything from retirement dinners to conventions and product launches—continues to flourish.

Pleasure, Recreation and Attractions

Notwithstanding its appeal to the business world, however, the Four Points Sheraton is also an ideal choice for accommodation for those who come to the area for pleasure, recreation and relaxation. Its downtown location and proximity to most of the area's major attractions is a definite boon to its tourist business.

In fact, the hotel, connected to the Market Square Shopping Centre and Kitchener Farmers' Market via an enclosed, glass skywalk, is just minutes away from the Centre in the Square Theatre, which draws internationally renowned performers and features a quality lineup of musicals, comedies, dramas, ballets and symphonies. Mennonite country and the quaint shops in the village of St. Jacobs are less than 20 minutes away, while Kitchener's finest boutiques and more than 65 local factory outlets are also close at hand.

Modern Guestrooms

As for the spacious and modern guestrooms, they contain all the standard features, plus extras such as en-suite coffee-makers, hair dryers and modem hookups.

Other Special Services

The Four Points Sheraton's emphasis on service is unmistakable, whether it's same day laundry and valet service, or the complimentary daily newspaper delivered to a guest's door or, the Starwood Preferred Guest Program, rated as the best hotel awards program in the world.

Extensive Fitness and Games Facilities

One of the more unusual aspects of the Four Points Sheraton, however, is an extensive fitness and play area that rivals some of the city's private clubs. It's substantial enough that some 300 fitness buffs who work and live in the downtown area own memberships that allow them daily access to all the facility has to offer. Squash courts and the latest in fitness equipment, for instance. Or regular aerobics classes run by certified instructors. The facility also includes an extensive play and recreation area that includes indoor mini-golf, table tennis, billiards, video games—even two five-pin bowling lanes.

Oktoberfest

The hotel plays host to numerous major events in the area. First and foremost is that one outrageous week in October. During this particular week, hotel staff shed their everyday garb for lederhosen and woolly knee socks, dirndls and garishly plumed Tyrolean hats. And an otherwise quiet lobby overflows with reveling locals and tourists dressed in similar attire. Its usually sedate ballroom is bedecked with appropriate decorations and is transformed into a giant festhalle of Oompah music, polkas, bratwurst, sauerkraut and a seemingly endless river of beer.

If you haven't guessed, the Four Points Sheraton is the official hotel of Oktoberfest, this area's annual and gigantic Bavarian culture/beer bash, and the largest Oktoberfest celebrations outside of Germany. It is here at the Four Points Sheraton that the annual pageant ball is held, and Miss Oktoberfest hopefuls from across North America vie for the coveted and nationally televised title. It is also here that dignitaries, tourists and locals converge following opening ceremonies.

But Oktoberfest isn't the only feather in the hotel's cap. Last year, the Four Points Sheraton also hosted such events as the Canadian Professional Figure Skating Championships,

A fully equipped meeting room with state-of-the-art audio-visual equipment.

and welcomed guests from around the world attending Engineering, High Tech and Agricultural conferences in conjunction with the region's two universities. Meanwhile, the National Hockey League's Toronto Maple Leafs stayed here for the first annual NHL Rookie Tournament, as they will this year along with the Buffalo Sabres and Carolina Hurricanes.

You Deserve Better

And don't think the Four Points Sheraton's motto "You Deserve Better" is confined to its guests. It is extended also to the community it serves as the hotel develops a growing reputation as a caring corporate citizen.

Not only is Kelly McCauley a Board member of the Kitchener Downtown Business Association and its concerted drive towards downtown revitalization, but the hotel is also a major sponsor of such organizations as the local symphony orchestra and the Canadian Cancer Society's famous annual Daffodil Tea.

And each year, hotel staff volunteer their time and efforts to organize at least two community-minded events, such as the annual Christmas luncheon for the homeless.

High quality amenities, mid-market prices and a staff whose emphasis on service extends to the community as a whole—all combine to make the Four Points Sheraton an ideal destination for business or pleasure. [■]

The Jacuzzi is an example of the extensive fitness and play areas offered to its guests.

increasing buying power and management efficiencies created with CHIP's large portfolio of hotels, CHIP Hospitality will optimize the financial performance of the REIT.

The rapid growth of CHIP REIT's portfolio (36 acquired hotel from June, 1997 to December, 1998) has slowed with the REIT now focusing on adding value and performance to its existing hotels. This year, CHIP REIT will invest $40 million to enhance hotels, brand key properties and strengthen its competitiveness in each market. In addition, through CHIP Hospitality, new performance enhancing processes and resources in the areas of sales and marketing, human resources development, purchasing, operations, franchising, accounting and information systems are being implemented.

"CHIP Hospitality is slated to grow through the management of CHIP REIT's new acquisitions, joint ventures and through the management of other full-service, independently-owned hotels in key locations across Canada and potentially the U.S.," says Minaz Abji, executive vice-president and C.O.O. for CHIP Hospitality. "We plan to grow by providing the best un-biased choices for the branding of the hotels we manage, and by offering independently owned hotels the opportunity to enter into low fixed, strong performance based management contracts. We are prepared to stand behind our track record." In 1998, CHIP Hospitality's management team and their portfolio of hotels, out-performed the Canadian Hotel Industry's average RevPAR by over 15 per cent. RevPAR (revenue per available room) is the standard measurement of performance in the hotel industry.

"Unlike most other hotel management companies, CHIP Hospitality is not limited, nor biased in branding decisions. With its unparalleled diversity of franchise relationships, CHIP Hospitality can strategically position and negotiate the right brand for the right hotel in the right marketplace," says David Thompson, Senior Vice President Sales and Marketing for CHIP Hospitality.

CHIP REIT (HOT.un:TSE Canadian Hotel Income Properties Real Estate Investment Trust), Canada's first hotel real estate investment trust, has internalized the management of the hotels in its portfolio with the creation of a subsidiary CHIP Hospitality. CHIP Hospitality currently manages 39 hotels as it is the exclusive management company of the 36 hotels owned by CHIP REIT and also provides management services for three other independently owned hotels.

CHIP REIT bought out the management division of Vancouver-based O'Neill Hotels & Resorts Ltd. which previously managed the 36 CHIP properties, and created CHIP Hospitality, a wholly owned subsidiary, that will now manage CHIP's hotels and thereby internalize profits and control. With a management team of leading industry experts,

(top) Crowne Plaza

(right) Festival Inn

In 1999 alone, CHIP Hospitality will open two new hotels and re-brand three others:

1. The independently owned $46 million development Westin Grand, Vancouver—Vancouver, British Columbia—opened April 1, 1999.

2. The independently owned $80 million development Westin Resort, Whistler—Whistler, British Columbia—opens December 1999.

3. The Radisson Hotel Calgary Airport—Calgary, Alberta (previously the New Crossroads Hotel)—opened May 1, 1999 with $4 million in renovations.

4. The Radisson Hotel and Conference Centre, Canmore—Canmore, Alberta, (previously the Greenwood Inn, Canmore) opened May 1, 1999 with $700,000 in renovations.

5. The Crowne Plaza Ottawa—Ottawa, Ontario (previously the Citadel Ottawa Hotel and Conference Centre) opening May 17, 1999 with $11 million in renovations.

CHIP Hospitality provides added value to the leadership and management of the hotels they manage. With specialists in hotel sales, marketing, development and design, franchising, operations, food and beverage, housekeeping, purchasing, systems and accounting, the CHIP Hospitality corporate team and hotel teams work closely to deliver incremental management value over and above the support offered by the brand or

management team of each hotel.

CHIP Hospitality is a newly-formed subsidiary of CHIP REIT (Canadian Hotel Income Properties, Real Estate Investment Trust) which is publicly traded on the TSE and is based in Vancouver, British Columbia. CHIP Hospitality is a multi-brand operator of hotels and currently manages 39 properties across Canada.

CHIP Hospitality is one of Canada's top five hotel management companies in terms of rooms managed and is currently managing almost 8,000 rooms. It is Canada's most diverse multi-brand operator of hotels managing such franchises as: Westin, Sheraton, Crowne Plaza, Radisson, Delta, Residence Inn by Marriott, Four Points by Sheraton, Holiday Inn, Quality Hotels, Best Western, Gouveneur and Ramada. The company also operates a number of successful independent hotels such as Mayfield Inn Suites in Edmonton, Alberta; Lethbridge Lodge, Alberta; Saskatoon Inn, Saskatchewan; the Festival Inn, Stratford, Ontario and the Gander Hotel, Newfoundland. The company has over 5,000 employees and almost $300 million in annual revenues. ▐◄

(top) Sandalwood Suites, (formerly Dodge Suites).

(left) Quality Inn

While they might be loathe to admit it now, there were plenty of detractors when Guelph's Holiday Inn was built 20 years ago amid a vast expanse of vacant and agricultural land far removed from the city's core.

But the decision to construct the original 80-room facility, the first Holidome, or atrium hotel, in Canada, has proven rather prophetic to say the least.

For one thing, business was so brisk when the hotel opened its doors that an additional 56 rooms had to be built just a year later. For another, the vacant land that once surrounded it quickly—and rather fortuitously—began to evaporate in the wake of the hotel's construction.

First came the adjacent four-lane Hanlon Expressway. Today, the Hanlon gives the hotel ready access to both the cities of Kitchener-Waterloo and major arteries such as Highway 401.

Other developments quickly followed, so that today the 136-room hotel is situated across the road from the vibrant Stone Road Mall with its more than 130 stores. It is abutted by one of the area's largest industrial parks as well as one of its predominant retail arteries.

But it's not merely the ideal

location that led to this mid-scale, full-service hotel's phenomenal 80 per cent occupancy rate last year. Rather, the decision to construct the hotel here in the first place is indicative of the type of vision that has driven this facility from the outset, a foresight that has enabled it to evolve and adapt with an ever-changing and highly competitive marketplace. The key factor one can't overlook is the hotel's obsession with customer satisfaction.

Outside driven—Inside inspired. That's the philosophy that motivates the 100-plus employees who staff this immaculate facility, recent recipient of the City of Guelph's Quality Award for the service sector.

Outside driven? That's a reference to the hotel's keen eye on emerging customer needs and expectations, the market savvy which allows it to keep one step ahead of its competitors. As for the Inside inspired part of the equation, that speaks to the unique contributions of each employee who is selected for his or her creativity, innovation and genuine dedication to customer service.

All of this has combined to create some high guest satisfaction ratings through the years. In fact, 90 per cent of the close to 60,000 people who spent at least one night here last year gave the hotel high marks. Not that this has created any complacency. Staff continually seek ways to improve the service they provide to their guests. Here, 100 per cent satisfaction is the ultimate goal.

The hotel is operated by Commonwealth Hospitality Ltd., a subsidiary of UniHost Corporation, the largest fully-integrated hospitality company in Canada. Initially conceived as a facility for the so-called leisure market, its five-storey, bathed-in-sunlight atrium, with its court-yard ambience, didn't disappoint. Here, visitors are encircled by lush greenery as they lounge around the indoor pool, loosen the kinks in the whirlpool or sauna, savour a cocktail in the cozy bar or enjoy a restaurant whose mouthwatering, country-style cuisine reflects an area that lays claim to some of the top